JUN 2015

CLOSING TIME

CLOSING

Prohibition, Rum-Runners, and Border Wars

DANIEL FRANCIS

TIME

 Douglas & McIntyre

CONTENTS

In the five months from July to November 1920 was packed the most dramatic episode in the history of liquor law enforcement in Ontario. It was the Spracklin case.

– ROY GREENAWAY, *Toronto Daily Star*

ELK LAKE
ONT

GREENAWAY OF THE *STAR*

■ NEAR THE END OF FEBRUARY 1931, THE Toronto crime reporter Roy Greenaway happened to be visiting Chicago when he read in the newspaper that Al Capone was making a rare appearance in a local courtroom. Hurrying around to the court, Greenaway found the notorious prohibition-era mobster, whom he had never met but with whom he had been trying to get an interview for several years, waiting for his case to be called. For a decade Capone, a native of New York City, had been the leader of Chicago's most successful crime syndicate, dealing in bootleg liquor, prostitution, extortion and various other illicit activities. Unlike most of his competitors, who preferred to operate in the shadows, Capone loved the spotlight and nurtured a high public profile. When they met, he and Greenaway provided a study in contrasts. The forty-year-old reporter was unassuming and mild-mannered. With his slim build, sandy hair and open, boyish face, he looked like a grown-up version of Tintin. Capone, on the other hand, was all sleek elegance and undisguised menace. He was wear-ing a diamond-studded watch chain draped across his vest and flashy rings on both hands. "The Capone that I saw," Greenaway wrote when recalling the encounter, "was over six feet tall, with shoulders wider than anybody else's in the whole court room. Out of a thousand people he would have attracted attention by his animation, his laugh, his raven-black brilliantined hair and eyebrows standing out against the ruddiness of his Miami-tanned face like patent leather against red paper. His large lips registered in the memory, as did the two scars on the left side of his face, one a pink welt a quarter of an inch wide extending from the sidebar almost to the corner of the lip, the other along the line of the jawbone."

When Greenaway introduced himself to "the czar of darkness," whose handshake he described as being "moist and soft like a sponge," Capone was friendly and willing to talk, though not about anything of any interest. The best quote came when the reporter asked the thirty-two-year-old gangster about his business in Canada.

On March 24, 1930, a year before Toronto reporter Roy Greenaway caught up with Al Capone in a Chicago courtroom, the 31-year-old mobster appeared on the cover of *Time* magazine, a sure sign of his place in the public imagination. During prohibition in the US, Capone organized a vast criminal network to supply illegal liquor to American consumers.

Although he denied it to Greenaway, Capone paid frequent visits to Canada to meet his suppliers. Unlike many of his cronies, he sought the limelight and was an energetic self-promoter. Capone went to prison for tax evasion in 1931 and by the time he got out in 1939 he was fatally ill from the effects of syphilis. He died in 1947, at age 48.

"I don't even know what street Canada is on," replied Capone, displaying "all the satisfaction of a wit who has spoken something memorable and was gloating over it." He had never even been to Canada, he claimed, abruptly ending the conversation.

■ ROY GREENAWAY WAS THE CHIEF chronicler of the prohibition era in Canada, the period between 1920 and 1933 when liquor flowed south across the border like water over a dam. The ineffectual "dam" was the Volstead Act, named for its sponsor Congressman Andrew J. Volstead of Minnesota. Passed by Congress in 1919, it was the law that implemented the 18th Amendment to the American Constitution banning the production, distribution and sale of "intoxicating liquors." When the Volstead Act came into force on January 17, 1920, Americans could no longer legally slake their thirst for spirits, beer or wine. For the next thirteen years, until the repeal of the Act in 1933, the whole of the United States was dry, at least in theory. But seldom has theory fallen so short of reality.

The Volstead Act was a US law but its influence in Canada was profound. American

politicians may have voted for prohibition but the American public had no intention of accepting it. Most people expected to go right on drinking in spite of the law and the source for most of their illegal liquor was Canada where distilleries, breweries and wineries continued to manufacture beverage alcohol. Of course, Canadians had their own complicated relationship with liquor, and with prohibition. During World War I the federal government banned the importation, manufacture and transportation of alcohol as a wartime measure, a ban that it lifted at the end of 1919. Meanwhile, the provinces passed their own prohibition laws. But each of the provincial laws had its own loopholes and none had the authority to deal with export or manufacture, which were federal matters. As a consequence, it was in the interstices of these various laws that the liquor traffic flourished, both within Canada and between Canada and the US.

Liquor smuggling went on all along the border from the coast of British Columbia to the outports of Newfoundland (technically not a part of Canada until 1949), but nowhere was the flow of illegal hooch quite so blatant and unrestricted as across the

A LEXICON OF LIQUOR

BLACK BOAT – a boat used for liquor smuggling; so-called because these vessels usually operated without running lights so as not to draw attention to themselves.

BLIND PIG – an illegal bar, usually catering to a working-class clientele; the term refers to the practice of displaying animals to attract customers.

BOOTLEGGER – someone involved in the illegal resale of liquor; the term refers to the practice of hiding a bottle in the top of a boot.

MOONSHINE – illegally distilled liquor.

RUM ROW – the fleet of coastal ships that lay outside the territorial limit of the US and were used to trans-ship smuggled liquor to smaller vessels for transport ashore.

RUM-RUNNER – someone involved in the illegal transport of alcohol across the international boundary, usually across water; rum came to be the generic term used for all types of alcoholic beverages.

SHORT CIRCUITING – the practice of illegally re-routing alcohol ostensibly meant for export back into Canada.

SPEAKEASY – a club or saloon where liquor was sold illegally, generally serving a higher class of customer than a blind pig; the term supposedly refers to the fact that customers were encouraged to "speak easy" so as not to attract attention from the law.

Prohibition had a vocabulary all its own. These customers are enjoying a round of beer at a "blind pig." This was a bar, usually catering to the working class, that served liquor illegally. Sometimes the bartender tried to get around the law by staging an attraction, such as a blind pig or some other animal. It was the attraction customers supposedly were paying for, not the "complimentary" drink they received to go along with it. Other explanations for the term have been proposed, including the suggestion that the bootleg liquor sold at these establishments caused blindness, or that police officers who were bribed to look the other way were known as "blind pigs."

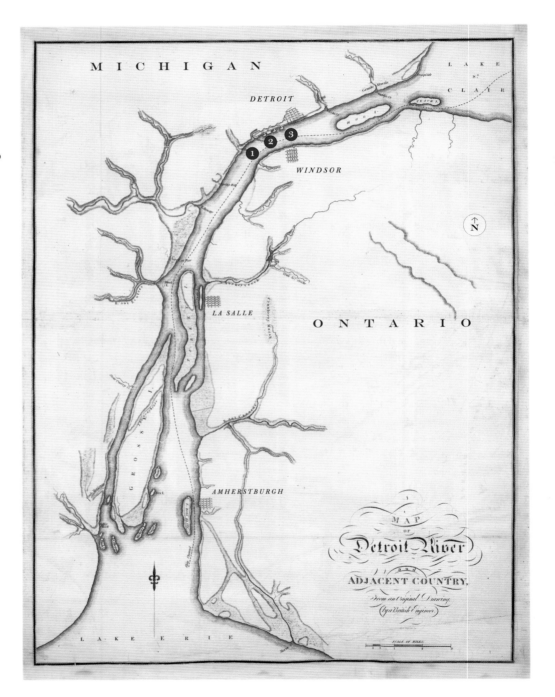

1 Ambassador Bridge 1929

2 Detroit-Windsor Tunnel 1930

3 Ferry Crossing

The Detroit River between the city of Detroit and Windsor, Ontario, separates Canada and the US but during prohibition it joined the two countries in a network of illicit liquor smuggling. The river travels south from Lake St. Clair 45 kilometres to Lake Erie; it is anywhere from 0.8 km to 4 km wide. Detroit is the largest city bordering Canada and it became the centre of rum-running once prohibition began. There were no bridges spanning the river until the Ambassador Bridge was finished in 1929, followed by the Detroit-Windsor Tunnel in 1930. Since ferry service was inoperable during the winter months, smugglers travelled across the frozen river by car, sled and wagon, or on foot. In some cases overloaded cars broke through the ice; unsalvaged cars from this era are still visible on the bottom of the river. The Detroit River, Lake St. Clair and the St. Clair River carried up to eighty percent of all liquor smuggled into the US during prohibition.

45-kilometre-long stretch of the Detroit River separating the Windsor, Ontario region from the state of Michigan. Michigan had gotten a jump on prohibition by introducing its own state law banning liquor sales almost two years earlier, making Detroit the first major city in the US to go dry. Given this head start, officials estimated that four-fifths of all the liquor smuggled into the US during prohibition used the so-called "Windsor-Detroit Funnel," amounting to an astonishing $40 million (US) a year.

This is where, in the summer of 1920, Roy Greenaway found his first big story.

It began in the pulpit of the Methodist church in Sandwich, Ontario, on the river south of Windsor, where the Reverend Leslie Spracklin began preaching fire and brimstone in the fall of 1919. Located just a stone's throw from the church was the Chappell House, a roadhouse owned by "Babe" Trumble. In the summer of 1920 Spracklin made the Chappell House the focus of his campaign to clean up the widespread abuse of liquor and the lax police enforcement that was allowing it to go on. Trumble and the pastor had known each other growing up in Woodstock, Ontario, and perhaps the bad blood went

back to some rivalry between them as boys. Public drunkenness, obscene language, disorderly conduct, flaunting of Ontario's temperance laws: these were all occurring nightly at the Chappell House, according to Spracklin, with the open collaboration of the local police. "The streets have become unsafe for our mothers, wives and daughters," he fulminated, "on account of the open debauch that is going on here."

The Chappell House was one of many raucous roadhouses that lined the frontage of the Detroit River south from Lake St. Clair. Most of these establishments had restaurants on the main floor, serving hearty dinners of chicken, fish and frog legs, with perhaps a ballroom or music hall for customers who wished to dance to the latest jazz. But the real profits came from the upstairs rooms where the liquor flowed and the gambling tables did a steady business. The Chappell House was even said to specialize in cockfights. All illegal, of course, but owners posted lookouts in the windows and the parking lots and at the first sign of a police raid the alarm bells sounded and all the incriminating evidence disappeared behind false walls and moveable furniture. When the police did

Prohibition in the US was by no means universally popular with Americans, as this protest rally in downtown Detroit indicates. But it became the law at midnight on January 16, 1920, and lasted for the next thirteen years.

enter, there was always a free drink waiting for them, along with a handsome bribe for looking the other way. When fines were imposed, they were accepted as another cost of doing business and the nightlife went on much as before. Many, if not most, of the customers were Americans who crossed the river by boat, tying up at the wharves that the waterfront watering holes provided. Located not far from the Chappell House was the Chateau LaSalle, owned by the flamboyant Vital Benoit, who used his own money to extend the streetcar tracks out from Windsor to deliver patrons directly to his door. Another well-known club owner was Bertha Thomas, proprietor of the Edgewater Thomas Inn. "Buxom, beautiful, full of personality," *Maclean's* magazine once called her. More importantly, she knew whose palm to grease and which politician to welcome to her exclusive upstairs gambling rooms. It was said that the carpets in the Edgewater Thomas Inn were so thick that when Bertha's spotters (one of whom was a schoolboy who sat in an upstairs window doing his homework while he watched for the cops) sounded the alarm the musicians and servers simply spilled the glasses directly onto the floor where the deep pile absorbed all the liquor, while the shelves of booze disappeared behind sliding walls.

This was the world of sin and corruption that the Reverend Spracklin set out to purify.

Spracklin's crusade was unpopular with the local town council and police, not surprisingly, since he threatened to expose them for incompetence, if not for outright graft. But he found a supporter in Toronto in the person of W.E. Raney, Attorney General in a provincial government dominated by the United Farmers of Ontario. Raney was a determined moral reformer who was infuriated by the open disregard for the prohibition laws that was being shown in the Windsor area. On July 30, 1920 he appointed a special squad independent of any other branch of law enforcement to clamp down on liquor violators. In charge of the new unit he placed Reverend Spracklin.

The combative preacher did not take long to exercise his new powers. On the evening of the day he was appointed he took a pair of inspectors and carried out raids at three roadhouses in his immediate neighbourhood. Raney soon provided him with two dozen reinforcements, some of whom were by popular account little better than thugs themselves. Spracklin and his men behaved like the gang of vigilantes they were. They carried guns and clubs, arrested people on the flimsiest of pretexts and when they needed to, filled out their own search warrants. As far as they were concerned, it was open season on anyone they suspected of being on the wrong side of the law.

More often than not, when the Spracklin flying squad made one of its raids Roy Greenaway was riding along with it. It was Greenaway who first started calling Spracklin the "fighting parson." He even moved into a room in the preacher's house. His newspaper, the *Toronto Daily Star*, was strongly in favour of prohibition. The reporter was also a friend of the Attorney General and the night before Raney announced his appointment of Spracklin and his special squad, he let Greenaway in on the secret. When the news broke in the pages of the *Star* the next day it was, the reporter wrote, "my first real scoop." From then on Greenaway pursued the story with daring and flair, and not a small amount of personal courage, riding along with both crooks and cops as they went about their business. It was, he said, "the most dramatic episode in the history of liquor law enforcement in Ontario." On August 3, 1920, he described a trip he made from Amherstburg, south of Windsor, with a gang of bootleggers in a large rowboat carrying fifteen cases of liquor across the river to Ohio. The closest liquor inspector lived twenty-five kilometres away, Greenaway was told, and there was only one local police officer. Bootleggers had a fleet of a hundred boats up and down the river, he reported, and more than a thousand cases of liquor crossed into the US every day. Greenaway himself favoured stricter enforcement and was appalled at what he thought was the lax attitude of inspectors and court officials. There was "a powerful element," he wrote, "which rejoices in the fact that Windsor is the widest open town in Canada and which particularly resents the ceaseless efforts of the 'fighting parson' to combat the organized liquor traffic." Bootlegging was widely tolerated in the border district, Greenaway complained; instead of reporting the rum-runners, most people envied their flashy cars and large incomes.

■ GREENAWAY'S REPORTS FROM THE front lines of the liquor wars were part of the "new journalism" as practised by the

Daily Star under its owner Joseph Atkinson and his dynamic city editor Harry Hindmarsh. Atkinson had joined the paper as publisher in 1899, recruited by new owners, a group of wealthy Liberal businessmen who wished to make it a party organ. The thirty-four-year-old Atkinson took the job, but only on condition that the owners allow him complete editorial independence. Under his direction – he eventually took complete control in 1913 – the *Star* gained steadily on its larger competitor, the *Telegram*, until by the early 1920s it had more readers than any of its local rivals and by 1930 it had the largest circulation of any newspaper in Canada. Atkinson was known as "Holy Joe" for his austere Methodist beliefs but there was nothing austere about the *Star*. It was one of the first papers to make the transition from bland party mouthpiece to a modern urban newspaper with contents aimed at a mass audience. More topical news, more sports, more gossip: these were some of the elements of the new formula. Atkinson's wife, "Madge Merton," edited the women's pages, and as a suffragist and a temperance supporter she put the *Star* at the forefront of both movements. Priced at just a penny,

RAZZLE DAZZLE

■ HARRY HINDMARSH JOINED the *Star* in 1911 and rose quickly through the ranks to become the paper's most influential editor. (It didn't hurt that he married the boss's daughter, Ruth Atkinson.) Hindmarsh is credited with applying a bit of "razzle dazzle" to the reporting style at the *Star*. It was a swarming style of journalism which saw squads of reporters and photographers let loose to get the story and get it first. "The army, the navy and the air force" is how veterans of the strategy described it. No expense was spared to follow every lead. "Reporters on out-of-town assignments had the expense accounts of minor Oriental potentates," observed one historian of the paper. "I really don't know whether these scoops pay or not," Joe Atkinson once said. "But they are a lot of fun." There was no house style. Hindmarsh encouraged his reporters to find their own voice, so long as it was urgent and breathless enough.

A couple of front pages from the *Daily Star* during the Hindmarsh-Atkinson era of razzle-dazzle journalism. As today, crime stories and politics dominated the news. By 1930 the *Star* had the largest circulation of any daily newspaper in Canada.

Joseph E. Atkinson was the innovative owner and publisher of the *Toronto Daily Star* and under his leadership it became the largest and most influential newspaper in Canada. Atkinson may have been a rich and successful businessman but many of his ideas were considered dangerously radical for their time – for instance, a tax on excess corporate profits – and conservative critics called his paper the *Red Star*. After he died in 1948 control of the paper passed to the trustees of the Atkinson Foundation, a major Canadian charity.

it was a paper for the man and woman in the street, not the boardroom. Atkinson was an enthusiastic crusader. He threw the paper behind any number of causes to improve life in Toronto. The *Star* campaigned to rid the city of flies, to pasteurize milk, to bring price fixers to justice, to send slum children to summer camp. And in turn, these campaigns earned for Atkinson the mass readership he was seeking.

Several fine writers got their start in the *Star*'s newsroom, including Morley Callaghan and Ernest Hemingway, and during the interwar period *Star* reporters like Gordon Sinclair, Gregory Clark and Fred Griffin were among the most famous journalists in North America. Eventually Roy Greenaway would join this august company but when he went down to Windsor to write about the Reverend Spracklin he had been in the news business for less than two years. It was, quite literally, an initiation by fire. What Greenaway soon discovered was that, not surprisingly, the bad guys were fighting back. Spracklin's life was threatened and twice a passing car sprayed his home with gunfire. Greenaway himself was shot at a couple of times as he went along on some of the raids. The

appointment of the fighting pastor had had the same effect as poking a stick into a hornet's nest. The hornets were aroused. "No exaggerations and calumnies have been spared by the liquor interests in their concentrated attack on Mr. Spracklin," Greenaway wrote. And it wasn't just the bootleggers who hated him. Spracklin's free-for-all tactics angered the local liquor inspectors who resented this Bible-waving Johnny-come-lately running roughshod through their territory. Early in November, Spracklin and the region's senior liquor inspector, M.N. Mousseau, appeared before the temperance committee of the provincial legislature in Toronto to air their differences. Mousseau pointed out that he never carried a gun and never engaged in the Wild West tactics of his rival. In response, Spracklin reminded the committee that he and his men in a short time had done more to subdue the liquor traffic than all the other inspectors combined. He demanded that the committee endorse his methods: "I don't want this miserable job for the enforcement of the [Temperance] Act, with all the risks I am taking and the disruption of my home, unless I can go back tonight or tomorrow feeling that I have the absolute confidence

Not surprisingly, manufacturers of alcoholic beverages fought back against the tide of prohibition with propaganda of their own. This series of cards bearing lithographic prints illustrates the idea that alcohol is a natural, healthful product, "the kindly fruits of the earth" as one card says. The cards were distributed by George Gies, a Detroit brewer, and were part of his campaign to show that, as opposed to hard liquor, beer was good for you. "Liquid bread," brewers liked to call it. Gies even went so far as to suggest that beer was a healthy drink for nursing mothers. Prohibition, so the argument went, violated the natural order of things.

> *"The whole place is deluged by a wave of cutthroats, thugs and pickpockets ... we'll have to answer some day for letting rum pour across the river as we have been doing."*
>
> – Reverend J.O.L. SPRACKLIN, Methodist minister of Sandwich

of this committee and the Government." J.D. Flavelle, chair of the Ontario Board of License Commissioners, agreed. "Extreme measures must be taken where there are extreme conditions," he told the committee. "I think the end justifies the means." At the end of the hearing, Spracklin won the support he was looking for.

But Spracklin and his political backers were asking for trouble. Just days after the session in Toronto, the pastor and some of his men barged their way into the Chappell House in the middle of the night. When "Babe" Trumble recognized Spracklin he reportedly confronted him with a gun. "It was his life or mine," the pastor told Roy Greenaway. Spracklin shot first. A bullet severed the femoral artery in Trumble's leg and he bled to death on the spot. Spracklin fled the scene, taking cover in a field across the street. "I have got into a little trouble, gentlemen," he told his men. Then he surrendered to police.

An inquest into the incident was convened immediately and the jury ruled that Spracklin had acted in self-defence. Free to continue his work as a freelance inspector, he instead resigned, telling Greenaway in an exclusive interview that he was going to go away with his wife for a holiday. "I am pretty well tired out," he said. He had certainly not changed his mind about the liquor traffic. "The whole place is deluged by a wave of cutthroats, thugs and pickpockets," he told a church meeting the day after his resignation. "We'll have to answer some day for letting rum pour across the river as we have been doing."

Spracklin might have faded from the front pages at this point but the Trumble family wouldn't allow it. They orchestrated a public petition demanding that the government investigate the shooting and on November 18, 1920, the Attorney General announced that the pastor would be charged with manslaughter. But the trial, which was held in Sandwich the following February, went against the Trumbles. The still-grieving widow, pregnant with her third child, testified that her husband had carried no gun that night and the police had never found one. But as Greenaway reported, Spracklin's lawyer was able to get key witnesses to admit that Trumble had been armed, that his wife had taken the gun from him as he fell and had hidden it and that subsequently one of his minions had dropped it in the Detroit River. Self-defence was proven and Spracklin got off for a second time.

■ SHORTLY AFTER HIS TRIAL LESLIE Spracklin resigned from his church. Pressured by persistent threats on his life, and also by accusations of sexual impropriety made by women in his congregation, he left Ontario, taking up a ministry in a small town in Michigan. For Roy Greenaway, on the other hand, the war was just getting started. Over the next dozen years he made the story his own. He rode along with the police as they gave chase to booze-laden speedboats on the Detroit River. He photographed smugglers as they dashed across the frozen river in the dead of winter pushing their illicit cargo on sleds ahead of them. He was sworn in as a special armed constable with the RCMP and granted honorary membership in the Michigan State Police. He ventured undercover into bootleg joints in Toronto and wrote stories exposing corruption in the federal customs department. Nothing sold newspapers like prohibition, and no one got the story as reliably as Roy Greenaway.

Prohibition is often thought of simply as

The Spracklin man-
slaughter trial filled the
newspapers. As the head-
line on the *Daily Star's*
front page suggests, the
jury was convinced of his
innocence and brought
in a verdict of not guilty
in no time at all. Instead
of jail, the crusading
Reverend retired from the
liquor wars and moved
to small-town Michigan.

The Spracklin case illus-
trates the "Wild West"
atmosphere that charac-
terized the early days of
prohibition along the
Ontario-Michigan border.

Toronto police arrest a man for illegal possession of alcohol on the day in September 1916 that the Ontario Temperance Act became law. The Act banned the sale and consumption of alcoholic beverages and closed all liquor retail outlets.

the period between 1920 and 1933 when the United States banned liquor. But Canada had its own version of prohibition, at different times, in different places and to different degrees. Attempts by moral reformers to rein in the consumption of alcohol resulted in a tangled web of laws across the country. At the local level, communities could vote themselves "dry" by passing ordinances banning the retail sale of liquor in a particular town or country. And many did. By 1900 in the Maritimes, for instance, two-thirds of the communities were dry. At the provincial level, it took the urgency of wartime to convince people that prohibition was necessary. With the exception of Prince Edward Island, which had introduced a province-wide liquor ban in 1901, and Quebec, which banned only spirits, all the provinces went dry at some point during World War I and remained so into the 1920s. In Ontario the provincial government enacted the Ontario Temperance Act (OTA), closing all liquor outlets and, with some exceptions, banning the sale and consumption of alcohol. The Premier, William Hearst, promised that once the war was over his government would hold a referendum to let the voters decide if the

OTA should be extended. In October 1919, by an overwhelming majority, Ontarians agreed that it should be. The world war convinced the federal government to act on the issue as well and in March 1918 it banned the manufacture and importation of liquor. For the next twenty-one months, Canada was as dry as any law could make it, which admittedly was not very dry. Distilleries and breweries continued to produce intoxicating beverages, bars and taverns continued to sell them and consumers continued to imbibe. It was against the law, but who really cared? Everyone was doing it and the police usually looked the other way.

Then, at the end of 1919, Ottawa lifted its ban and allowed producers to manufacture liquor for export, either to a foreign country or to another province where prohibition was not in force. From a Canadian perspective, in other words, it was perfectly legal to send booze south of the border. Not just legal but highly lucrative. "But I'll tell you, everybody was doing it," recalled bootlegger Blaise Diesbourg, supplier to Al Capone himself. "Everybody took the stuff across, because it was the best way to make some good, fast money. Take it under your coat on a ferry, a

Long before prohibition, governments were attempting to control the consumption of alcohol. This "Act for regulating the manner of licencing public houses and for the more easy convicting of persons selling spirituous liquors without licence" dates back to colonial times in Upper Canada (Ontario).

First Parliament, ⎱ LAWS OF THE PROVINCE OF UPPER CANADA.
Third Session. ⎰   34th Geo. 3. C. 12. A. D. 1794.

AN ACT

For Regulating the manner of Licencing Public Houses, and for the more easy Convicting of Persons selling Spirituous Liquors without Licence.

WHEREAS, the provisions contained in a certain Ordinance of the late Province of Quebec, passed in the twenty-eighth year of his Majesty's Reign, intituled, " An Act or Ordinance for the better security of the Revenue arising on the retail of Wine, Brandy, Rum, or Spirituous Liquors," have been found inconvenient ; and whereas it is expedient to make other and more easy regulations respecting the granting of Licences to Houses of Public Entertainment ; Be it enacted by the King's most excellent Majesty, by and with the advice and consent of the Legislative Council and Assembly of the Province of Upper Canada, constituted and assembled by virtue of and under the authority of an Act passed in the Parliament of Great Britain, intituled, " An Act to repeal certain parts of an Act passed in the fourteenth year of his Majesty's Reign, intituled, " An Act for making more effectual provision for the Government of the Province of Quebec, in North America, and to make further provision for the Government of the said Province," and by the authority of the same, That the said Act or Ordinance shall be and the same is hereby repealed.

II. *And be it further Enacted by the Authority aforesaid,* That from and after the twentieth day of March next, no Licence shall be granted to any person to keep an Inn or Public House for the purpose of vending Wines, Brandy, Rum, or other Spirituous Liquors ; unless he shall first have obtained a Certificate of his being a proper person to keep an Inn or Public House, from the Magistrates of the Division wherein he resides, or is about to reside, to be granted to him as herein after specified, and all Licences which shall be hereafter granted to the contrary hereof shall be null and void.

III. *And be it further Enacted by the Authority aforesaid,* That for the said purpose, it shall and may be lawful for the Magistrates acting in each and every Division of the several Districts of this Province, to limit the number of Inns and Public Houses in their several Divisions, and to appoint a day of public meeting in each Division in either of the two last weeks in the month of March in every year, at a convenient place within their several Divisions, by a Warrant under their hands and seals, or under the hands and seals of any two of them, at least ten days before such meeting, directed to the High Constable or other Peace Officer, requiring him to give notice in the most public manner of such intended meeting, and then and there to hear and receive applications from all such persons as desire to take out Licences for opening Inns or Public Houses within their said several Divisions, and the said Magistrates shall, upon hearing and receiving any application from any person praying to have a Licence granted to him, enquire into the life, character and behaviour of the person so applying, and if it shall appear to the greater part of the Justices then and there assembled, that it is expedient to increase the number of Inns or Public Houses, and that the party applying is a sober, honest and diligent man, and a good subject of our Lord the King, they shall then and there grant a Certificate accordingly, under the hands and seals of any two of them, which

A

Margin notes:
Preamble.

Recital of an ordinance passed 28 Geo. 3.

The same repealed.

Certificates to be obtained by persons, previous to their being licenced.

The number of inns may be limited by the magistrates.

Meeting of magistrates, annually in March, in order to determine upon applications for licences.

A certificate from the magistrates so assembled, shall serve as a warrant to obtain a licence.

Canadian brewers profited by exporting their product into the US once prohibition was proclaimed there. At the same time their business suffered from the imposition of "dry" laws in Canada. Prior to prohibition there were more than one hundred breweries operating across the country. Most were small, family-owned businesses serving local or provincial customers. By 1924 the number of breweries had fallen to sixty-four as during the decade many of the small operations failed or were absorbed into larger companies.

2 ·

3 ·

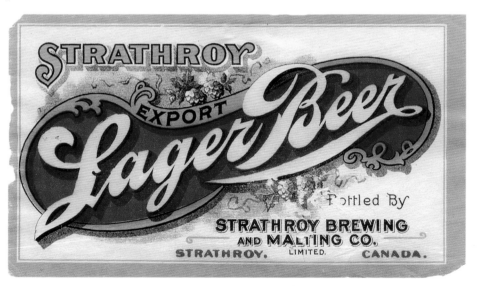

PROHIBITION WINDFALL

1 ·

1 • A label from the Strathroy Brewing and Malting Co., founded by Mathew Bixel in the town of Strathroy, not far from London, Ontario.

2 • The Lake Ontario Brewing Company in Portsmouth, Ontario, near Kingston, was one of more than two dozen breweries that were manufacturing for export during the prohibition era in the province.

3 • In 1909 the Montreal Brewing Company was absorbed into National Breweries Ltd., a new corporation including most of the breweries in Quebec.

4 • John H. Sleeman began brewing beer in western Ontario during the 1830s.

5 • The Silver Spring Brewery operated in Sherbrooke, Quebec, from 1897 to 1928.

6 • The Bixel Brewing and Malting Company began operations in Strathroy, Ontario, in 1859 and moved to Brantford thirty years later. The brewery remained in the Bixel family until 1944.

7 • Reinhardt Brewery, founded in Toronto in 1881, is thought to have been the first to produce lager beer in the city.

8 • The Hamilton Brewing Association formed in 1903 as a coalition of three Hamilton-area breweries, including H. Kuntz.

9 • Prince Albert Breweries was one of several Western Canadian breweries owned by Fritz Sick (1859-1945), credited with developing Old Style Pilsner beer. The Sick interests were eventually purchased by Molson Inc.

4 •

5 •

6 •

7 •

8 •

9 •

Hand Brand was a type of cheap liquor manufactured by bootleggers in the French islands of Saint Pierre and Miquelon and sold during prohibition in the Acadia region of Maritime Canada. It was so strong that it was usually diluted with water before drinking.

Like French-speaking Catholics in Quebec, Acadians tended to be against prohibition and not overly concerned about the illegal activities of smugglers. This artifact is the end piece of one of the crates in which bottles of Hand Brand were shipped.

A truck loads up with cases of liquor at an Ontario warehouse across the river from Detroit in 1925. Until 1930, exporting liquor from Canada into the US was legal so far as the Canadian authorities were concerned.

The American side of the border was a different matter, however, and smugglers employed all sorts of ruses to sneak their cargoes into the US.

couple of cases in a rowboat, any way you want. But me, I went into it in a big way. I took it across the ice, eight hundred cases of whiskey and beer, and it was like a highway out there – the cars going back and forth – and no one to stop you." It wasn't just organized crime and large hotel owners who were in the business. Anyone with $15 could import a case of whisky from Quebec and sell it across the river for as much as $120. There wasn't any job in Canada that paid that much for so little work. Much of the liquor left Canadian shores completely legally, ostensibly documented as exports to Cuba, Mexico, the French islands of Saint-Pierre and Miquelon or some other foreign destination. Of course, once it left the docks, with the appropriate paperwork in hand and federal taxes paid, there was no telling where it might end up. There were many stories of rowboats filled with whisky and beer setting off for "Cuba" from the Canadian side of the Detroit River and arriving back just a couple of hours later for another load! "We all knew what was going on," recalled one customs agent, "and we knew that stuff was all going to Detroit, but it wasn't our jurisdiction. Once it left the docks and left

Canadian waters, there wasn't a thing we could do. If it got diverted, that wasn't our fault." Bootleggers, manufacturers, rum-runners, crooked cops and inspectors all made a nice living from the liquor traffic. And so did the federal government. It has been estimated that during the 1920s proceeds from export taxes on liquor amounted to twenty percent of all government revenue in Canada. In 1929 alone the tax on alcohol brought in twice as much revenue as the income tax. There were a lot of people with no incentive whatsoever to enforce the law.

Joseph Atkinson had decided to make it the business of the *Daily Star* to expose the fraud. The Spracklin case was just the beginning. The *Star* and its weekly national magazine supplement, the *Star Weekly*, kept up a steady drumbeat of sensational articles. In February 1923, Greenaway and a photographer named Benjamin Rogers were on the frozen Detroit River south of Windsor trying to get photographs of the smugglers in action. The river all the way from Lake St. Clair to Amherstburg was lined with warehouses where the liquor was stockpiled waiting to cross to Michigan. During the summer, shipments moved

Aviation was still in its infancy but intrepid smugglers used aircraft to transport liquor across the border. Blaise Diesbourg supplied Al Capone himself, loading former World War I fighter planes with twenty-five cases of whisky per trip. The enterprise had its risks. Here a squad of American prohibition enforcement officers are unloading a cargo of contraband whisky they have seized from a captured airplane on a frozen lake.

across on speedboats – "Neither government had boats fast enough to catch more than a glimpse of the bootleggers' shadows," Greenaway wrote in the *Star* – but during the winter the gangs had the more laborious job of hauling the cases of booze across the ice. As Greenaway and his companion approached the river in their battered old Ford an amazing scene presented itself. "The boats! Do you see them?" Rogers asked.

There before our astounded eyes were the boats, on runners, loaded down to the gunwales with kegs and cartons of beer.

They were spaced out at approximately hundred-yard intervals.

We soon counted twelve, and more were shooting out from the shelter of the canals on the Canadian side. The men shoving and dragging them across the ice looked like pirates in their toques and high rubber boots.

A rail line serviced the warehouses, carrying the liquor right to the wharves for loading. When the smugglers saw Greenaway and Rogers they quickly shooed them away. "Take pictures?" one of them said. "Absolutely not! We want no publicity around here."

Moving down the river the two journalists

scrambled across the ice, took cover behind a ridge of dirt and began snapping photographs of the boat sleds as they passed. It was broad daylight, Greenaway noted, yet there were no police in sight and at least seventy-five men out on the ice. "I'm just going over to buy some fish," cracked one of them as he passed. Throwing the camera in the back of the Ford, they just managed to drive off before a gang of angry goons came looking for them. That Greenaway and Rogers were in some danger was proven by another incident involving a photographer from a local newspaper, the *Border Cities Star*. Horace Wild was chased down by members of a "rum gang" he was photographing near Amherstburg and lowered into the river with weights attached to his ankles before cooler heads prevailed and the thugs satisfied themselves with destroying the film (they thought; Wild actually had more film hidden away and his photographs appeared in the newspaper after all). Running liquor across the border may seem like an adventure to us now, but it was deadly serious for those who engaged in it.

The liquor traffic attracted many small-time operators who were just trying to make

LEFT An American enforcement official closes down a Detroit bar at the onset of prohibition in the US in 1920.

BELOW Smuggling a cargo of liquor across the Detroit River seemed like an easy way to make some money but the adventure did not always end well. In this case a truck has broken through the ice, dumping its cases of illicit booze, while onlookers survey the damage. Note that the quartet in the rear are wearing ice skates.

ABOVE **These beer labels belong to three of the country's venerable brewing companies. The Walkerville Brewery was founded by Hiram Walker in Walkerville, Ontario, in 1885. It operated under its original name until 1943 when it was absorbed into Carling Breweries. The old brewery building was demolished in 1956. Carling dates back to the early nineteenth century when local farmer Thomas Carling began selling his home-brewed beer on the streets of London, Ontario. During the 1930s Carling became part of the Brewing Corporation of Ontario (later Canadian Breweries Ltd.), a conglomerate organized by the business tycoon E.P. Taylor. Labatt, also based in London, Ontario, was founded in 1847 by John Labatt, an Irish immigrant to Canada, and grew to become the largest brewery in the country.**

LEFT **Construction workers building an addition to a hotel in Tavistock, Ontario, in 1894 take a beer break. Drinking on the job was common in colonial Canada but by the time this photograph was taken it was frowned on. Nonetheless, the hotel owner (second from right, holding a tray) obviously felt that his crew deserved some liquid refreshment.**

ABOVE One of the gangs active in the Detroit-Windsor area was led by the Licavoli brothers, Yonnie and Pete. The Licavolis took over the illegal liquor business from the Purple Gang and controlled much of the smuggling across the Detroit River from Ontario into the US. In 1927 Yonnie (shown here second from right with some of his criminal associates) was convicted in Windsor, Ontario, of carrying a concealed weapon and served three years in a Canadian prison. Soon after his release he became embroiled in a gang war in Ohio and in 1934 ended up back in jail where he remained for the next thirty-seven years. Pete was more fortunate. He was arrested seven times for murder but the charges never held and he retired a wealthy man to a ranch in Arizona.

OPPOSITE Detroit police display cases of illegal liquor seized in a raid in the city during the 1920s. Most of this contraband would have originated north of the border and been shipped into the US, quite legally until 1930, by some of Canada's most respectable brewers and distillers.

a dishonest buck, but most of it was controlled by the various gangs that ran Detroit's gambling, extortion, narcotics and prostitution rackets. One of the most notorious outfits was the Purple Gang, a particularly vicious group of mobsters with roots in the city's Jewish community. Members of the gang did some smuggling themselves but they preferred to simply hijack the cargoes that other rum-runners were bringing across. The Purples did not hesitate to eliminate any opposition that got in their way and witnesses to their crimes were too intimidated to testify against them. Even the mighty Al Capone in Chicago decided it was better to arrange for the gang to be his supplier than to try to set up his own Detroit operation. The Purples had their rivals, of course; there was too much liquor flowing across the river for just one gang to handle. The roughest competition came from the River Gang, led by the Licavoli brothers, Yonnie and Pete, and there were several others, including the Sugarhouse Gang, the Westside Mob and the Vitale gang. The bloody turf wars between these rival gangs filled the pages of the Detroit press with murder and mayhem.

■ THE CANADIAN SIDE OF THE RIVER DID not have gangs as organized or as brutal as the Purples but the Windsor area did have its liquor kingpins. Chief among them was Harry Low, an auto industry machinist turned pool hall owner. With the onset of prohibition, Low began selling bootleg liquor to his patrons and soon graduated to the export trade, becoming a major supplier to the Purple Gang. His operation shipped whisky from Montreal through the Windsor-Detroit Funnel into the US and in 1924 was part of a syndicate that purchased the Carling brewery in London, Ontario, and began producing beer for export as well. Despite the illegality of his business, Low was not embarrassed by it. Quite the reverse: he lived an ostentatious lifestyle which included the luxury mansion he built for himself in Walkerville. Devonshire Lodge had oak parquet floors, leaded windows, a stunning spiral oak staircase in the main hall and an undulating roof of shingles imported from England and meant to resemble the thatched roof of a Cotswold cottage. Low lost most of his assets in the Depression and died a penniless recluse. The house, a Walkerville landmark, was

CANADA'S WHISKY

■ ALL WHISKY IS MADE FROM A mash of water and cereal grains – corn, wheat, barley – but in Canada, rye became the signature grain. It was brought here by early Dutch and German settlers and proved to be suited to the northern climate. Distillers began adding it to the mash to give Canadian whisky a distinctive taste – a little bitter, a little spicy. Whisky made without rye became known as common whisky. In time Canadian whisky and rye whisky became synonymous, even though today rye is added to the blend mainly for flavouring and corn is now the predominant grain. With a higher starch content than other grains, corn yields more alcohol and is easier to distill. In contrast to Canadian whisky, Scotch and Irish whiskey were usually distilled from barley, and in the US, bourbon was made from a mash derived mainly from corn. The quality of a whisky depends in part on the ageing process. From 1890 it was the law that all Canadian whisky had to be aged for two years before it could be sold. Since 1974 the law has required a minimum three years of ageing, which is the same as Irish whiskey and Scotch.

By late in the nineteenth century, ageing in oak barrels had become an important part of the distilling process. Ageing allowed the whisky to mature and develop more subtle flavours. Gooderham & Worts advertised that its "Special" Rye matured in oak casks for ten to twelve years. "Special" Rye, one of the company's best-selling brands, was used as an ingredient in a variety of cocktails.

2

G & W SPECIAL

Famous for over 100 years. Its delicate bouquet and mellow flavour is due to being allowed to mature in oak casks for ten years or more. 25 oz. and 13 oz.

Famous for Over 100 Years

CANADIAN RYE COCKTAIL
In a large glass or shaker put:
  2/3 G & W "Special"
  1/3 Italian Vermouth
  Dash of Angostura Bitters
Shake well with crushed ice and strain into cocktail glass.
Serve with a piece of twisted lemon peel.

MILLIONAIRE COCKTAIL
Fill shaker 1/3 full cracked ice:
  1 white of a fresh Egg
  Two dashes of Cointreau Triple Sec.
  1 tsp. of Grenadine
Add G & W "Special" to required strength.

RYE SOUR
Half fill shaker with ice:
  2/3 G & W "Special" Rye Whisky
  Juice of one Lemon
  1 tsp. of Sugar
  1 liqueur glass of rich Cream
Shake well, strain into cocktail glass and serve with cherry.

3

In 1900 the Hiram Walker Company erected this giant illuminated sign at its Walkerville plant across the river from Detroit. The sign, which read "Distillery of Canadian Club Walkerville," advertised the company's best-selling brand of rye whisky.

It was the largest electrical structure of its kind in North America, measuring 36.5 metres across and 23 metres tall.

owned for many years by Paul Martin Sr., a long-serving cabinet minister under prime ministers Mackenzie King, St. Laurent and Pearson, and the father of former Prime Minister Paul Martin.

Walkerville is a story in itself. It was a community built on liquor. Hiram Walker was a Detroit grocer who expanded into the distillery business. Recognizing the rising popularity of the temperance movement in the US, he moved from Detroit across to Canada where he purchased a large piece of land on the river east of Windsor and in 1859 established the Windsor Distillery and Flouring Mill. Walker milled flour and raised livestock but his main interest was making whisky. One of his better brands was Club Whiskey, a premium brand aged seven years in oak barrels. It was popular in the finer men's clubs and restaurants south of the border, and became even more popular after Walker added the word "Canadian" to the name, making obvious the brand's country of origin and distinguishing it from Kentucky bourbon and Scotch whisky. Canadian Club was soon the best-selling whisky on the market and the renamed Hiram Walker and Sons was the largest distiller in Canada.

Walker's company headquarters was a mock Renaissance Florentine palace. It was one of the most extravagant office buildings in the country. Rooms were finished in marble, oak and mahogany and included a barbershop and a gym. At the outset of prohibition the company added a wing to the original building, including a swimming pool in the basement and living apartments upstairs. Surrounding this merchant castle was the townsite, the eponymous Walkerville, where almost all of Walker's employees lived. It was a company town: families banked at the Walker-owned bank, washed in water provided by the Walker-owned utility, travelled across the river to Detroit using the Walker-owned ferry company and relied on a police force and a fire department paid for by Walker. In 1891 he built his own railway as far as St. Thomas, a distance of more than 100 kilometres, which helped to attract other businesses to the community. Walker was the unchallenged monarch of his own principality and by the time he died in 1899, at the age of 83, his town was a major industrial centre.

Prohibition turned out to be both a windfall and a curse for Hiram Walker's sons, who took over direction of the company

following their father's death. The company made a lot of money supplying the river of booze flowing into the gin joints and speakeasies in the US. But eventually the illicit traffic attracted attention from law enforcement and crusading politicians, attention that made life uncomfortable for respectable businessmen like the Walker brothers who were unused to working on the wrong side of the law. During the first six months of 1926 a special parliamentary committee in Ottawa was looking into irregularities in the customs and excise department. It was dubbed the "smuggling committee" and revealed all manner of embarrassing details about the lax regulation of liquor traffic, including the fact that distillers had avoided paying millions of dollars in sales and excise taxes. The committee's report led to the sacking of the minister of customs and the appointment of a full-blown Royal Commission to further investigate the department. As it became evident that the dirty linen of the distilling industry was going to be aired in public, the Walker brothers thought the time had come to separate their family from impending scandal. At the end of 1926 they sold Hiram Walker and Sons for $14 million, which

WALKERVILLE, ONTARIO, CANADA. THE HOME OF "CANADIAN CLUB" WHISKY.

ONE OF THE BOTTLING ROOMS.

A vintage postcard shows employees at work at the Hiram Walker bottling plant. Originally distillers sold their product in barrels. Walker innovated by putting his product in bottles, each one bearing the name of his company and the brand of whisky it contained. Walker's whisky was the first Canadian-made whisky sold around the world.

In 1898 he applied for, and received, a Royal Warrant which enabled the company to put Queen Victoria's coat of arms on the label of its Canadian Club brand. This came about because the Queen's physician had suggested she stop drinking wine and champagne and instead use Canadian Club whisky as an aid to digestion. Canadian Club continued to hold its Royal Warrant through successive British monarchs.

according to one estimate was about half what the company was worth. For the first time since the town was established, Walkerville's founding family was out of the liquor business.

The new owner of Hiram Walker was Harry Hatch. Hatch had got his start in the liquor business as a young man tending bar in his father's hotel saloon in Deseronto, Ontario. When Ontario introduced prohibition he moved to Montreal to get into the mail-order business and eventually joined the Canadian Industrial Alcohol Company (CIAC), owned by Sir Mortimer Davis, founder of Imperial Tobacco and one of Montreal's leading business tycoons. Hatch ran the illicit side of CIAC's operation, organizing a fleet of fishboats, known as "Hatch's Navy," to smuggle liquor across Lake Ontario to the US, and profits soared. In 1923 Hatch purchased his own distillery, Gooderham & Worts, located on the Toronto waterfront. Three years later, when he bought Hiram Walker, he combined the two operations as Hiram Walker-Gooderham & Worts. It was the middle of prohibition and the industry was thriving. The Bronfman brothers were organizing Distillers Corporation, soon

to be Seagram's, in Montreal and Mortimer Davis, who included in his business empire the Corby Distillery Company near Belleville, Ontario, had built a new plant capable of producing ten thousand gallons of whisky a month. Ahead of these well-known rivals, Hiram Walker-Gooderham & Worts was the largest distiller in the British Empire and the *Toronto Daily Star* crowned Harry Hatch the "King of the Canadian Distillers."

But there was trouble ahead. Profits may have been soaring but patience on both sides of the border was wearing thin with the flagrant disregard for the law. The Royal Commission on Customs and Excise held public hearings across the country during the winter of 1926–27 and the revelations were embarrassing and incriminating. Once the commission's final report was in, with admissions by the distillers that they had been violating American law by exporting booze across the border, the US Treasury Department felt it had to act. Thirty Canadian companies faced indictments, including Harry Hatch's operation. Suddenly one of the richest men in Canada was a wanted felon in the US. The impact of the American indictments was negligible, however,

James Worts and his brother-in-law William Gooderham established a grist mill at York (now Toronto) near the mouth of the Don River in 1831. Six years later the operation added a distillery and began producing its first whisky. From these humble beginnings Gooderham & Worts grew to be the largest distillery in the world, shipping its product to markets across the globe from its lakeside wharves. Then came hard times, in the form of World War I when the company was forced to contribute to the war effort by switching to the production of acetone. After the war came prohibition and in 1923 the company was purchased by Harry Hatch who soon combined it [1926] with Hiram Walker and Co. to form Hiram Walker-Gooderham & Worts. The distillery remained in business under different ownership until 1990 when finally it closed. Afterwards the buildings were used as a set for filmmaking and the site is now the centre of an arts and heritage district on Toronto's waterfront. The lithograph below is an advertising poster showing the distillery in 1896 when the company was in its heyday.

GOODERHAM & WORTS, LTD.
TORONTO, CANADA.
CANADIAN RYE WHISKY

The Ferry Landing, Windsor, Ont., Canada.

compared to the stepped-up efforts by law enforcement to get control of liquor smuggling. Beginning in the fall of 1927 the Ontario Provincial Police began raiding the export docks along the Detroit River, seizing liquor worth millions of dollars. On both sides of the border, enforcement agencies increased the frequency of their patrols and the number of boats deployed throughout the Great Lakes to intercept the smugglers. Finally, in June 1930, Prime Minister Mackenzie King's government gave in to public pressure, and to American threats, and amended the Export Act to stop the legal export of booze to the US. Most of the export docks around Windsor closed. Smuggling continued on a reduced scale, but the heyday of the Windsor-Detroit Funnel was at an end.

■ FRUSTRATED AT ONE LOCATION ALONG the border, the liquor traffic simply shifted to another. As enforcement picked up along the Detroit River and the Great Lakes, suppliers moved their activities offshore to the tiny French island of Saint-Pierre in the Atlantic, south of Newfoundland. Not surprisingly this is where we catch up with Roy Greenaway, arriving by boat from Sydney,

Nova Scotia, late one afternoon in the fall of 1931 to write a series of articles for the *Daily Star*. Reporters were not welcome on the island which, along with its neighbour Miquelon, was the last remnant of France's once mighty North American empire. Since their economy at this point relied almost entirely on smuggling booze into the United States, publicity was the last thing the Saint Pierrais wanted. Greenaway was masquerading as an advertising agent and once he'd passed the scrutiny of the border officials he stashed his camera and film in a hole in the mattress in his hotel room. As he and his wife strolled about the island, surreptitiously collecting information, they could see signs of the liquor traffic everywhere: in the crates of whisky piled high on the quayside; in the rum boats being loaded for the trip to American waters; in the heaps of empty liquor boxes littering the front yards of the houses for use as firewood; in the dredges in the harbour that were just finishing the improvements that would allow larger freighters to arrive from Canada and Europe with their holds full of booze; in the people making burlap bags to carry the bottles. Always the resourceful reporter,

ABOVE **A colour postcard from 1920 shows the ferry landing at Windsor, Ontario, looking across the Detroit River. For much of the 1920s docks along the river were the conduits for shipments of illicit liquor being smuggled from Ontario into the US via Detroit. Finally, beginning in 1927, the so-called "export docks" were shut down, dealing a blow to the liquor traffic and forcing the smugglers to find other ways to move their product.**

OPPOSITE **A couple of young helpers pack bottles of Scotch whisky into burlap sacks outside a liquor warehouse on the island of Saint-Pierre. The sacks would have been reloaded onto schooners heading to destinations along the Eastern Seaboard of the US. Liquor smuggling provided jobs and income for an island economy in dire need of both.**

These photographs capture the ingenuity shown by individuals smuggling liquor past the border guards.

LEFT TO RIGHT **A woman carries two or three bottles in a kitchen apron; the term "bootlegger" derived from this practice of concealing a bottle in a boot-top; a modified backpack carries a half dozen bottles of whisky, though surely the clinking must have given him away; this burlap girdle carried as many as twenty bottles beneath a coat.**

Greenaway managed to convince a foreman to let him inside one of the storehouses. "The warehouse was like a mine whose veins of ore were endless rows of whiskey bottles," he wrote. The nondescript building contained a half million dollars worth of product, ranging from bottles of champagne and flasks of Peter Pan whisky to kegs of rye. "Every room in the island is packed with liquor," Greenaway's informant told him. "There are not enough warehouses to hold all the bottles. That's the trouble at present. So the liquor firms rent rooms wherever they can in the people's homes, and even spaces in their cellars."

Greenaway soon had his story but as he sailed away from "this lonely citadel of the rum-runners" he must have realized that he was witnessing the end of an era. He had been tracking prohibition for more than a decade. He had been shot at by border patrols on the Detroit River, travelled with the smugglers, toured the rollicking "blind pigs" and speakeasies of Jazz Age Toronto, exposed corruption in the federal customs department, even met Al Capone. But now the curtain was coming down on the drama and as a good journalist Greenaway would have known it. For one thing, Capone was in

jail, convicted on five counts of tax evasion in the courthouse where Greenaway had met him earlier that year. More importantly, everywhere across Canada the provinces had decided to abandon their vain attempts at prohibition in favour of some form of government-controlled liquor sales (except for Prince Edward Island, which would not get wet until 1948). Liquor had been available at government-run stores in Greenaway's home province of Ontario for four years already. The Americans were also getting set to reconsider their dry experiment. Sixteen months after Greenaway watched the rum-runners loading their cargoes at the bustling waterfront docks on Saint-Pierre, the US Congress in February 1933 repealed prohibition and America was wet again.

In retrospect, prohibition seems like a colossal mistake. Like today's "war on drugs," it began as a popular crusade that was supposed to cleanse society of a widespread evil. But also like today's war on drugs, the cure turned out to be worse than the disease. Prohibition created not a sober, law-abiding population but an opportunity for larceny on a grand scale. That's how it's remembered, and rightly so. But what's sometimes

forgotten is the reform impulse from which prohibition sprang. It wasn't a conspiracy hatched by a few moralizing zealots: prohibition was voted for by majorities of ordinary people who thought they knew how to improve society. Furthermore, it was not introduced thoughtlessly or in a hurry but only after many decades of debate. Since at least the 1830s large numbers of Canadians had been worrying about the impact of alcohol on family life and social mores. World War I gave government the excuse it was looking for to implement the policy, but the idea of prohibition – and temperance, its milder sibling – had been around for a very long time. The story of prohibition has deep roots in Canadian history. It represented a stunning attempt to use the law to transform entrenched social behaviours. No other public issue was voted on as often, or remained on the public agenda for so many years. And even as it ended in failure, the relevance of prohibition is still debated today as Canadians discuss the merits of legalizing the use of so-called recreational drugs. Apparently prohibition is the single social issue that just won't go away.

The American artist Charles Deas (1818–67), was known during his lifetime particularly for his depictions of Aboriginal culture in the American West. He spent the last twenty years of his life in a mental hospital in New York where he continued to paint, though his subject matter became increasingly dark and moody. In this 1838 oil painting, "Walking the Chalk," a drunkard in a tavern is challenged to walk a straight line. In colonial Canada, excessive drinking was common and the tavern was an important social centre. As time passed, however, some Canadians became concerned about the effects of excessive drinking on family life and public morals. Scenes such as the one depicted in the painting were seen less as harmless fun and more as indicators of social pathology. These concerns gave rise to the temperance movement and, ultimately, prohibition.

Your committee are firmly convinced that the traffic in intoxicating liquors ... is detrimental to all the true interests of the Dominion, mercilessly slaying every year hundreds of her most promising citizens; plunging thousands into misery and want; converting her intelligent and industrious sons, who should be her glory and strength, into feeble inebriates, her burden and her shame; wasting millions of her wealth in the conscription of an article whose use not only imparts no strength but induces disease and insanity, suicide and murder...; in short, it is a cancer in the body politic...

– Report of a Committee of the Canadian Senate, 1874

THE COLD-WATER ARMY

■ IN THE EARLY NINETEENTH CENTURY, alcohol was as pervasive in the everyday life of Canadians as coffee is today. In the years before Confederation not many things united the colonies that made up British North America, but a love of strong drink was one of them. In many places booze was more accessible and safer to drink than water or milk. Liquor was a medicine, a currency, an incentive to work and a reason to relax, a warmer in the winter and a cooler in the summer, a release and a consolation. It was a part of the daily routine, and the daily diet. Wine and beer were consumed with every meal, including breakfast. Votes were bought and sold for a glass of grog. Doctors prescribed spirits as a tonic to prevent disease and aid in digestion. New mothers were even told that it encouraged their breast milk to come in. Workers received a midday pick-me-up from their employers. Soldiers drank a daily ration to keep up their courage; in his history of the War of 1812 Pierre Berton figured that in most battles "the combatants on both sides were at least half drunk." Barn raisings and other communal work parties were fuelled by alcohol; neighbours might lend a helping hand but they expected generous drink in return. Every town of any size had its own brewery, and taverns were the community centres of the colonial world.

Drinking to excess was not as frowned upon as it is today. Some of the country's leading politicians overindulged, with little negative impact on their popularity. The most notorious drunkard was the first prime minister, John A. Macdonald, whose prolonged binges only seemed to endear him to voters. When a heckler once challenged him on the subject, Macdonald famously remarked that the country preferred him drunk to George Brown, one of his political rivals, sober. And Macdonald was no exception. In British Columbia, Frederick Seymour, governor of the colony from 1866 to 1869, was a known alcoholic. When he died aboard a naval vessel in Bella Coola while on a mission to the north coast the official cause was dysentery but the

■ Scottish-born Alexander Keith came to Halifax when he was twenty-two years old and three years later, in 1820, he was operating his own brewery, which has been in business ever since. As beer became increasingly popular in the Maritime colonies Keith's business prospered and he became one of the leading merchants in Nova Scotia, expanding his activities to include banking, insurance and public utilities. He also served three terms as mayor of Halifax and was a prominent Freemason, rising to become grand master of Nova Scotia. Keith died in 1873. His palatial home, Keith Hall, built ten years before his death, still stands in downtown Halifax, as does the adjoining brewery building.

ship's doctor reported the governor's "inordinate craving" for brandy, an entire bottle of which he had consumed shortly before his passing.

Cheap rum from New England and the West Indies was a staple import to all the colonies, along with French brandy and Scottish whisky. Colonial governments relied on the duties collected from these imports to provide much of their revenues. During the 1830s in Nova Scotia and New Brunswick, for instance, import duties on alcohol provided between a quarter and a half of all government income. Beer manufacturers tended to be local and many breweries familiar to Canadians today got their start in colonial times: John Molson in Montreal in 1786, Alexander Keith in Halifax in 1820, John Sleeman in St. Catharines, Ontario, in 1836 and Thomas Carling and John Labatt in London, Ontario, during the 1840s. Brewers and distillers were among the most prosperous merchants in British North America and some of Canada's largest fortunes have been based on the booze trade.

For all the rum that entered the colonies legally, just as much was smuggled in to avoid paying the duties, especially in the

Maritimes and especially in the port communities such as Halifax, Saint John, Liverpool and Lunenburg where rum found a ready market among the fishermen, millhands, loggers, soldiers and sailors who congregated there. In Halifax, an eighteenth-century clergyman famously asserted, "the business of one-half of the people was to sell rum, and of the other half to drink it." The city "is nothing less than a great big Rum shop," wrote one temperance advocate in 1862, a reference to the two to three hundred licensed drinking spots then flourishing in the city. Toronto, too, acquired a reputation as a free-drinking town. By the mid-1840s its population of twenty thousand was served by one hundred and fifty unlicensed watering holes, two hundred licensed taverns and five hundred beer shops. "Absolute drunkenness ... abounds to a greater extent in Toronto than in any town of the same size in America," reported one visitor.

In Western Canada it was liquor that led to the creation of one of the country's most enduring icons, the Mounted Police. In the 1870s whisky peddlers had become such a blight on the Prairies that Prime Minister John A. Macdonald created a special police

BELOW A beer wagon delivers barrels of beer from the Molson's Brewery in Montreal, c. 1908. Molson's was founded by John Molson who had immigrated to Quebec in 1782 at the age of eighteen and became involved in different businesses with family friends, including a brewery in Montreal. After he turned twenty-one, Molson took over the brewing operation and developed it as the basis of a family business empire. One of the city's leading industrialists, Molson was also part owner of the first steam-boat on the St. Lawrence River, the *Accommodation*, launched in 1809, and invested in Canada's first railway. Today Molson's is the second-oldest cor-poration in Canada after the Hudson's Bay Company. Since 2005 it has been the Canadian division of Molson Coors Brewing Company, the world's seventh-largest brewer.

RIGHT In 1847 John Kinder Labatt, a farmer near London, Ontario, sold his land and purchased a share in a brewery owned by his friend Samuel Eccles. Labatt & Eccles prospered and when his partner died John Labatt took over sole ownership, changing the name to London Brewery. When he showed an interest in the business, John K.'s youngest son, also named John, was sent to appren-tice to a brewer in West Virginia where he learned the secrets of making India Pale Ale. Returning to London, John Jr. took control of the brewery when his father died, changed the name to Labatt and Company and developed India Pale Ale as its signature brew.

MURDER IN THE CYPRESS HILLS

■ ON JUNE 1, 1873, A GROUP OF drunken American wolf hunters attacked an Assiniboine camp near one of the whisky posts in the Cypress Hills in southern Saskatchewan. The wolfers thought, wrongly as it turned out, that the First Nations had stolen their horses. Dozens of Assiniboine men, women and children were killed and wounded before the survivors could escape. (One wolfer died.) The incident became known as the Cypress Hills Massacre and when word of it reached the outside world it accelerated efforts to deploy a mounted police force to the Northwest. Attempts to extradite five of the Americans from the US failed. Eventually two of the men were arrested in Canada and went on trial in Winnipeg but by this time the trail of evidence had gone cold and the case was dismissed.

Alcohol played a crucial role in the development of Western Canada since it was to curb its abuse that the North West Mounted Police was created in 1873. Members of the new force marched west from Manitoba to drive the whisky peddlers from the Plains. One of the new police posts was Fort Walsh, established in the Cypress Hills, the centre of the illegal liquor traffic. It was near here that the police negotiated with the great American Sioux leader Sitting Bull when he crossed the border into Canada in 1877 following his defeat of General George Custer at the Battle of Little Bighorn. The government closed and dismantled Fort Walsh in 1883 as part of its policy to remove the First Nations from the Cypress Hills. Today the area is a National Historic Site.

OLD FORT
F. Walsh - 8

N.W.M.P. CAMP – FORT WALSH – 1878
NEG 266

force to deal with the problem. In October 1873 one hundred and fifty recruits assembled at Lower Fort Garry in Manitoba to begin training. A railway scandal drove Macdonald from office that month but his successor as prime minister, Alexander Mackenzie, agreed that the new force, christened the North West Mounted Police, was necessary and in the spring of 1874 a great caravan of men and supplies left Lower Fort Garry heading west across the Plains toward "Whoop-Up Country." The new police force managed to eradicate the illegal liquor traffic and impose British justice on the frontier. This was a seminal moment in the creation of the country and it came about largely because of liquor.

Across the mountains in British Columbia the sale or trade of alcohol to Aboriginal people likewise began with the arrival of the earliest fur traders. In 1854 the Executive Council of the colony of Vancouver Island banned the exchange of alcohol with the First Nations. Twelve years later, when the island colony joined with mainland BC to form a single colony, prohibition became even more stringent. But the illegal liquor traffic flourished. The Pacific coastline was simply too long and too convoluted to allow

effective policing. The "whisky" that was traded, of course, was watered down and adulterated with all manner of noxious additives so that it was often more poison than pleasure. Authorities complained that the liquor traffic was the ruination of the Aboriginal people. "Among the greatest obstacles in the way of elevating the Indian there is none more potent than the present illicit whiskey traffic," declared Israel Wood Powell, the superintendent of Indian Affairs, in his first report in 1873. When it could catch them, the navy impounded the vessels, dumped the cargo overboard and fined the masters. But enough smugglers got away with it that they were willing to take the risk.

A more benign view was taken of drinking in white settlements, where alcohol abuse was rampant. In the mid-1860s Victoria had one hundred and forty-nine licensed drinking establishments for a population of fewer than three thousand people. Vancouver, soon to be the province's principal city, actually was founded by a saloon keeper; "Gassy" Jack Deighton arrived in Burrard Inlet with a barrel of whisky in 1867 and opened the Globe Saloon to cater to thirsty workers at a nearby sawmill. Deighton gave his name to

Four Cree warriors, including the great chief Big Bear, or Mistahimaskwa, trade their beaver pelts at Fort Pitt, Saskatchewan in 1884. The younger man seated in front is Sky Bird or King Bird, one of Big Bear's sons. In exchange for the furs the Cree would have received a variety of trade goods, but not liquor, which had been outlawed since the arrival of the North West Mounted Police a decade earlier.

The brothers Ed and Gordon Temple step up to the bar in a Victoria saloon, c. 1914. In turn-of-the-century British Columbia, alcohol consumption was twice the national average.

Gastown, the little community that grew up around his establishment. By 1900 Vancouver boasted forty-seven hotels, twelve saloons, seven liquor stores and a variety of illegal "blind pigs," and in the province generally, liquor consumption was twice the national average. In BC's resource-based economy, bars were where men came to trade gossip, let off steam and look for their next job in the mines, fish canneries or lumber camps.

■ IF LIQUOR AT TIMES SEEMED TO BE the lifeblood of colonial Canada, it was the tavern, saloon or public house where most people got their transfusion. Open twenty-four hours a day, seven days a week, these were the corner coffee shops of their day. Taverns were licensed to sell alcoholic beverages by the glass for consumption on the premises, as distinct from their near relatives the beer-house, which sold only beer, and the liquor shop, which was a retail outlet for booze by the bottle. In 1801 there were just over one hundred taverns in Upper Canada (Ontario); by mid-century the number had exploded to 2,723. In the countryside thirsty travellers could find a

tavern every few kilometres along their route; in the towns there was one on almost every corner. Naturally they varied in quality and clientele, from the backwoods cabin to the rough-hewn working man's hangout to the finest urban establishments with marble bartops and sumptuous meals.

And like the modern coffee shop, taverns served a myriad of purposes. Life was hard in pre- and early-industrial Canada. Hours of work were long, up to twelve hours a day for many people, six days a week, with few holidays. Jobs in the factories, mills and workshops were physically demanding, unrelieved by labour-saving machinery. The domestic situation of urban workers offered little respite. Houses were cramped, ill-heated in winter and ill-ventilated in summer. Epidemic diseases such as diphtheria, smallpox, typhoid and tuberculosis killed many. In Montreal, to take the worst example, a quarter of all newborn babies died before they reached a year of age, making it the unhealthiest city in North America. Out of doors there were few parks or playgrounds and the streets reeked of garbage and horse dung. Leisure time came in short, intense bursts; little wonder that many

JOE BEEF'S CANTEEN

■ ONE OF THE MOST NOTORIOUS taverns in the country was Joe Beef's Canteen opposite the Bonsecours Market near the waterfront in Montreal. Joe Beef's was owned by an Irishman named Charles McKiernan, a former quartermaster in the British army who took his discharge and settled in Montreal with his family in 1868. The tavern he opened soon after was officially called The Crown and Sceptre but everyone knew it as Joe Beef's, the nickname McKiernan had acquired while serving in the Crimean War. He catered to a boisterous mix of dock workers, factory hands, soldiers, sailors, beggars and thieves. McKiernan proudly called his establishment the "Great House of Vulgar People" and the respectable citizens who disdained it as a centre of vice and criminality would have heartily agreed. Standing at his place behind the bar, McKiernan was an imposing figure. A newspaper reporter described the "easy style of his dress, corduroy trousers strapped by a military waist-belt, a white shirt rolled up to the shoulders [which] showed off the extraordinary development of his muscles ... A slight black billy-goat adorns his chin, and when he talks with anyone he is continually twisting it with his fingers." McKiernan dispensed food, drink and worldly wisdom in equal parts but the Canteen was far more than a simple tavern. The unemployed came there looking for a day's work, the hungry to seek a handout and the curious to see the tame bears that were kept beneath a trap door in the cellar. McKiernan was the champion of the working-class population of the city. He used his notoriety to speak out in support of improved social services and better pay and working conditions on the waterfront. "Always the poor man's friend" was how the *Gazette* newspaper described him when he died suddenly of heart failure in 1889.

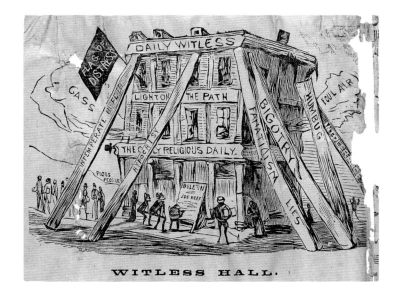

Cartoonist John Henry Walker makes fun of the *"Daily Witless"* for its "pious," "humbug," "hypocrisy," "fanaticism" and other extreme pro-temperance views. The *Montreal Witness* was a daily newspaper that regularly attacked Joe Beef and he was not reluctant to answer back. One of the bears at the canteen was named Jenny Dougall after John Dougall, editor of the *Witness.*

Alcohol was as much a part of everyday life in early Canada as milk or coffee. Here a group of farm workers take a beer break at Langenburg, Saskatchewan, c. 1899.

workers chose to spend such time in the convivial atmosphere of the tavern.

Along with strong drink, customers could find something to eat, a room for the night, even female companionship, if that was what they were looking for. Taverns were stagecoach depots where journeys began and ended and travellers purchased their tickets. In the absence of a community hall or courthouse, they hosted political meetings and polling stations, auctions, inquests and trials. Itinerant physicians and dentists examined their patients there while lawyers consulted their clients and salesmen displayed their wares. When the circus came to town, or a boxing match, or a horse race, taverns were the favoured venue. And when there was nothing doing at all, patrons came simply to sit and read the newspaper or chat with their neighbours. In short, taverns were far more than drinking establishments, which perhaps explains why attempts by moral reformers to portray them as dens of iniquity and to shut them down met with such limited success.

■ DRINKING, AND DRINKING TO EXCESS, may have been widespread in colonial

Canada but it was not condoned by everyone. Some observers – religious leaders, social reformers, women's groups, doctors and others – began to argue that British North America needed a great reformation in its drinking habits. Originating in the United States, this temperance movement spilled north across the border during the late 1820s. Temperance societies, often called lodges, formed spontaneously in tiny hamlets and large urban centres alike. Itinerant orators travelled from community to community preaching the cause. Many of these meetings had the trappings of a religious revival, featuring fervent preaching about hellfire and salvation. Churches took a leading role in the campaign; drinking was a sin, temperance the path to the new millennium. Temperance, wrote John Dougall, the long-time leader of the movement in Montreal, "would prepare the way for the time of universal peace, purity and happiness promised in the Gospel." By 1832 there were one hundred organized lodges in Upper Canada, while in 1843 one quarter of the adult population of Saint John, New Brunswick, belonged to a temperance society. Temperance newspapers such as the

A SERMON IN SIX CARTOONS. No. 4.

Ye brewers are reconciled with drink;
And ye Devil, with tempting smile,
Proffers ye curse from ye hand of Death
And ye victims doth beguile.

PRESENTED WITH FRANK LESLIE'S ILLUSTRATED NEWSPAPER.

The Church of England Temperance Society (CETS) was the most prominent temperance group in Britain in the late-nineteenth century and was active in Canada as well. Its associated Woman's Union concentrated its efforts on eradicating drunkenness among working-class women.

The CETS also operated "inebriate homes" for men and women suffering from alcoholism. Pendants like these were distributed to members who had taken the pledge and would probably have hung around the neck on a ribbon.

Canada Temperance Advocate in Montreal and the *Temperance Telegraph* in New Brunswick had huge circulations. Initially the movement tolerated moderate drinking – one Quebec society's idea of temperance was taking no more than six glasses of liquor per day – but as the enthusiasm spread so did support for the ideal of total abstinence or teetotal (the word comes from the slogan "capital T total abstinence").

Temperance may have been imported from the US but it would not have taken root if conditions in British North America had not made people receptive. During the decades following the War of 1812, the Canadian colonies received a flood of immigration that threatened to overwhelm their social institutions. Many of the newcomers were impoverished Scots and Irish, driven from their own countries by poverty and starvation. The colonial legislatures took small steps to assist them, but jobs were hard to come by and few of the immigrants were prepared for the back-breaking toil of life on a backwoods farm. Workhouses and poorhouses overflowed with new arrivals who could not support themselves. Jails filled with the destitute who turned to petty theft to survive. Successive disease epidemics overtaxed the limited public health facilities. In June 1832, for example, an epidemic of cholera, originating with a group of new arrivals at Quebec City, swept up the St. Lawrence into Upper Canada. By the time the disease burned itself out in October, several thousands had died. In 1847 it was typhus that arrived with the immigrant ships. Twenty percent of the people who left the British Isles for Canada that spring did not live to see the winter.

Ultimately, this mass migration would prove to be the making of Canada. At the time, however, to established residents at least, it seemed to challenge the orderly society they had created for themselves in the colonies. In response to this perceived social crisis, many people jumped on the temperance bandwagon, finding in the movement an answer to the problems that plagued the colonies. The social and economic costs of excessive drinking seemed to be everywhere visible: in abandoned women, broken families and increased criminality and mental illness. The churches were prominent in the new movement but temperance was as much secular as it was religious.

The *Canada Temperance Advocate* was established by the Montreal Temperance Society in 1832 and at one point had the largest circulation of any newspaper in Canada. Newspapers like the *Advocate* were among the most effective ways the temperance movement spread its message.

A cartoon by John Henry Walker depicts an unlikely scene: the temperance champion John Dougall sharing a glass with Prime Minister John A. Macdonald, a notorious binge drinker. Walker (1832–1899), an Irish immigrant to Canada, was an engraver whose illustrations appeared in the leading publications of the day.

Members of the "cold-water army" were not all dour religious fanatics. Many were progressive thinkers, social reformers who were not wrong to identify alcohol abuse as the cause of much human suffering and social dislocation.

The two faces of the temperance movement – religious and secular – were evident in Canada East (Quebec). On the secular side was John Dougall, a Montreal businessman and journalist. Dougall was animated by his own Congregationalist faith but it was as a publisher that he made his mark on the temperance movement. In 1835 he took over as editor of the *Canada Temperance Advocate*, the organ of the Montreal Temperance Society. Much more than a special-interest journal, the *Advocate* claimed more readers than any other newspaper in the country. As the paper's editor, Dougall enjoyed a leadership position in the movement, not just in Quebec but across British North America. His efforts extended well beyond the editorial office. He toured widely in Quebec and Canada West (Ontario), meeting with local groups, speaking on temperance issues and distributing books and pamphlets. In 1846 Dougall injected his enthusiasm for

moral reform causes into the mainstream press by establishing the *Montreal Witness*, initially a weekly paper but from 1860 a daily. The *Witness* was a family newspaper, by which was meant a journal that included articles of interest to women and even children as well as the usual news of the day and political items. It was the first Canadian newspaper sold on the street by newsboys for a penny a copy (many of the same newsboys who found accommodation at Joe Beef's Canteen). Politically non-partisan, the paper was stridently anti-Catholic, at least the conservative, ultramontane form of Catholicism that Dougall thought was dominant in French-speaking Quebec. So obnoxious did the Roman Catholic hierarchy in the province find the *Witness* that in 1875 the Church actually banned the paper; no Catholic was allowed to buy it, sell it, read it or advertise in it. By the early 1870s the *Witness* was the second leading paper by circulation in Canada, after the *Toronto Globe*. Though it was read by many, the paper was not a big money-maker. Dougall cut himself off from major sources of revenue because he refused to accept advertising for liquor, patent medicines or popular

Brewers countered the negative propaganda of the temperance movement by emphasizing the healthful qualities of their product. Consumers were assured of the nourishing benefits of drinking beer.

Here, labels from three different breweries suggest that individuals convalescing from illness or suffering from invalidism should prescribe themselves a strong beer such as stout.

Manufacturers argued that alcohol was a tonic that restored strength and cured whatever ailed you; "as rich and nourishing as fresh cream," one advertisement promised. It cured indigestion, stimulated the brain and generally toned up the system.

CAISSE DE BIENFAISANCE DE TEMPERANCE.

SECTION ST JACQUES.

entertainments. His papers were vehicles for temperance and other moral reforms more than for profit.

For several years during the 1840s Dougall's counterpart as the most vociferous temperance crusader in the French-speaking community was Charles Chiniquy, a fiery Catholic priest. Quebec was experiencing a resurgence of the Roman Catholic Church following the political rebellions of 1837-38 and some members of the clergy, led by the reactionary bishop of Montreal, Ignace Bourget, saw an opportunity to take a leadership role in the temperance movement. Father Chiniquy had seen the results of excess drinking while serving as a hospital chaplain in Quebec City and in 1840 he established a temperance society in the parish of Beauport where he was the curé. That same year a popular religious awakening swept the province, sparked by the oratory of Charles Forbin-Janson, a visiting bishop from France. Wherever he went Forbin-Janson sponsored the creation of temperance societies and tens of thousands of new converts to the cause became members. By the time Forbin-Janson visited Beauport the enthusiasm for temperance was at a fever pitch. Father Chiniquy organized

a vast procession of ten thousand chanting followers culminating in the raising of a column in support of temperance. It was one of the largest public celebrations ever held in the province and it launched Chiniquy on his own fire-and-brimstone crusade as the leading temperance promoter in French-speaking Quebec. In 1848 Bishop Bourget invited Chiniquy to Montreal to preach for temperance. In the next eighteen months Chiniquy reportedly delivered five hundred sermons and won an astonishing two hundred thousand converts to the cause. His picture hung on the walls of parishioners' homes and his arrival in a parish prompted mass jubilation, parades and cannonades. His speaking style was vehement and dramatic; he spelled out in graphic detail the awful effects of alcohol abuse and called on his listeners to come forward to take the pledge of total abstinence. For Chiniquy, "the canker of intemperance" was a threat to the very survival of a healthy, industrious, pious French Canadian culture.

Then, at the height of his popularity, it all collapsed. The charismatic Chiniquy was a difficult personality. Arrogant, ambitious, vain, not to mention sexually indiscreet –

the Church had tried to hide his repeated transgressions with female parishioners – he chafed at any attempt to rein in his activities. He was so popular with the laity that the Church hierarchy found him difficult to control but in 1851 an opportunity presented itself to ship him off to Illinois to work with Canadians who had emigrated there. Predictably his dynamism got him into trouble with the local bishop, against whom he rebelled, and eventually Chiniquy was excommunicated. (He converted to Presbyterianism and returned to Canada to preach against the Roman Catholic Church, for whom he was a constant thorn in the side until his death in 1899.)

■ WHETHER IT WAS PROMOTED AS A PATH to personal salvation, a necessity for cultural survival or a response to the social problems of crime, poverty and family dysfunction, the temperance movement swept British North America. It has been estimated that at the height of Father Chiniquy's crusade, half the population of Quebec had taken the pledge. This enthusiasm was echoed in the other colonies as well. At mid-century, abstinence seemed to be the new normal.

One of the earliest attempts to organize temperance activists into a national organization was the Canada Temperance Union, founded in Toronto in February 1869. The Union stood for "total abstinence" and even worked to create a temperance political party, but its national ambitions were unrealized and a year later members decided to confine their efforts to Ontario.

Across British North America more than half a million people swore off liquor. Alcohol use was far less prevalent on the job and a new atmosphere of restraint had come to prevail. Preferences had changed as well, as the popular taste gravitated away from strong spirits toward beer. But for temperance enthusiasts, the glass continued to be only half full. Working men still gathered in saloons where they wasted their incomes and neglected their families. Too many converts fell off the wagon back into a life of dissolution. Alcohol still played too large a role in the daily life of Canada, at least in the opinion of the cold-water crusaders.

When it began, temperance, as the word implies, was a call for moderation. Early campaigners frowned on the consumption of spirits but beer and wine were tolerated. As time passed, the movement became more totalitarian, requiring its adherents to forsake alcohol in all its forms. Teetotalling became the objective. At this point temperance was still a voluntarist movement, requiring individuals to abandon the bottle of their own free will. Voluntarism failed to bring about an alcohol-free society, however, and by mid-century many adherents

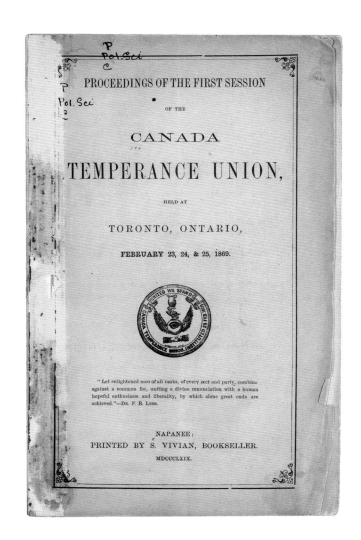

PROCEEDINGS OF THE FIRST SESSION

OF THE

CANADA

TEMPERANCE UNION,

HELD AT

TORONTO, ONTARIO,

FEBRUARY 23, 24, & 25, 1869.

" Let enlightened men of all ranks, of every sect and party, combine against a common foe, uniting a divine renunciation with a human hopeful enthusiasm and liberality, by which alone great ends are achieved."—DR. F. R. LEES.

NAPANEE:
PRINTED BY S. VIVIAN, BOOKSELLER.
MDCCCLXIX.

"VOTE WET FOR MY SAKE!"
"VOTE DRY FOR MINE!"

This cartoon from a newspaper in Victoria, BC, shows a brewer urging voters to "vote wet" while a mother with three children (and a husband presumably at the bar) urges the prohibition option. Once local option became a possibility, prohibition was on the ballot in communities across the country. Coupled with repeated province-wide plebiscites, and the national plebiscite of 1898, there has probably not been another public issue in Canadian history on which voters were asked to make a choice so often.

began agitating for legislation to enforce complete prohibition. Most politicians were reluctant to get involved in the issue. They did not want to alienate wealthy brewers and distillers and the many voters who still liked a drink. Nor did they want to give up the substantial revenues from taxes, licence fees and import duties. As a result, public officials hoped to placate the temperance movement with partial measures such as limiting the number of licences for taverns and liquor stores, regulating the hours of operation and enforcing Sunday-closing laws.

Here and there across the country, however, governments made the first faltering attempts to legally prohibit the consumption of alcohol altogether. The first attempt by a colonial government to ban booze occurred in New Brunswick. In 1852 the Sons of Temperance, British North America's leading temperance organization, sponsored a sizeable petition of nine thousand signatures demanding an end to the importation of alcoholic beverages and presented it to the New Brunswick Assembly. Inspiration came from south of the border where in 1851 the State of Maine had enacted a tough prohibition law, the first in the US, and several

other states and territories were following suit. Carried along by what appeared to be the popular will, the Assembly passed the requisite bill which became law at the beginning of 1853 and New Brunswick went dry. But not for long. Colonists turned out not to be as enthusiastic for prohibition in practice as they had been in theory. The act was ignored, circumvented and violated with impunity. The mayor of Saint John, the largest city, simply refused to acknowledge its authority. Seeing that the liquor traffic flourished outside the law, the Assembly withdrew the act after a year. But temperance supporters, led by Samuel Leonard Tilley, one of the most influential politicians in the colony and a senior official in the Sons of Temperance, would not let the matter rest. When a new faction, led by Tilley, took control of the Assembly a prohibition bill passed for a second time, coming into effect on the first day of January 1856. But just as ardently as Tilley and the Sons supported prohibition, so did its opponents abhor it. The result was a period of violent unrest that verged on anarchy. Neighbours turned into spies, friends into enemies. Members of the Sons took to patrolling the streets like

vigilantes, looking for violators, while rioters protested the bill. Tilley was burned in effigy, his life threatened. So many people violated the law that prosecutions were impossible. Finally a shaken colonial governor stepped in, forcing an election in which Tilley lost his seat and a majority of anti-prohibition candidates – their opponents called them "Rummies" – were elected. Within days the new Assembly repealed prohibition for a second time by an almost unanimous vote.

The New Brunswick experience seemed to show the wisdom of acting incrementally. Full-blown prohibition would not be tried again anywhere in Canada for several decades. But the desire for temperance was still strong, and colonial legislatures (and later, provincial ones) were willing to take small steps to slake it. Licences to retail alcohol or operate a tavern became more expensive and harder to obtain. Local governments limited hours of operation. But the main compromise solution was local option. In 1864 the Canadian legislature passed the Dunkin Act, providing for local option in Canada East (Quebec) and West (Ontario). According to the law, local governments – counties and municipalities – could opt to

The Sons of Temperance was an American fraternal order that opened its first Canadian branch in 1847 in New Brunswick. Ultimately it became the most influential voice for prohibition in pre-Confederation Canada.

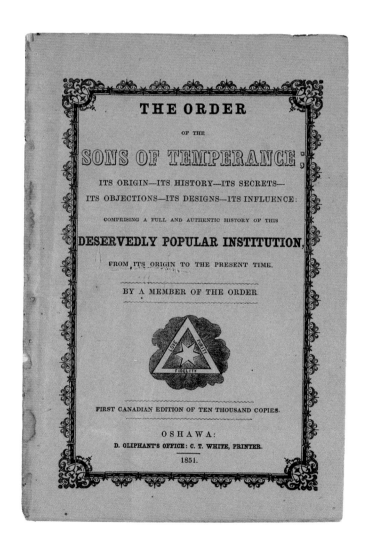

THE ORDER

OF THE

SONS OF TEMPERANCE,

ITS ORIGIN—ITS HISTORY—ITS SECRETS—
ITS OBJECTIONS—ITS DESIGNS—ITS INFLUENCE:

COMPRISING A FULL AND AUTHENTIC HISTORY OF THIS

DESERVEDLY POPULAR INSTITUTION,

FROM ITS ORIGIN TO THE PRESENT TIME.

BY A MEMBER OF THE ORDER.

FIRST CANADIAN EDITION OF TEN THOUSAND COPIES.

OSHAWA:
D. OLIPHANT'S OFFICE: C. T. WHITE, PRINTER.
1851.

■ As a teenager, Samuel Leonard Tilley apprenticed as a druggist in Saint John. It was the temperance movement that led him into politics. As a member of the Sons of Temperance he rose to become "most worthy patriarch," the highest position in the organization. First elected to the New Brunswick legislature in 1850, he made repeated attempts to promote laws banning alcohol. But he was not a one-issue politician. He supported railway development and union with the other colonies. Twice premier of New Brunswick, he was a crucial voice convincing voters to accept Confederation. It is said that he suggested the word "Dominion" to describe the new federation. In 1867 he joined John A. Macdonald's first cabinet in Ottawa. Later he twice served as lieutenant governor of New Brunswick. He died of blood poisoning in 1896 at the age of seventy-eight. This photograph shows him in 1873.

Alcoholic beverages, taken in moderation, were widely believed to have medicinal benefits. Doctors dispensed a variety of tonics and extracts to improve digestion and invigorate the system. As well, the temperance movement made an exception for "near beer," beer with a low alcohol content, much like today's "lite" beer.

1 • Hofbrau Liquid Extract of Malt was recommended for "the nursing mother, the invalid, the convalescent, and … the athlete" as being "gentle, stimulating and nutritive." Reinhardt & Company was a Toronto brewery.

2 • The British American Brewing Co. manufactured this malt extract to treat whatever ailed you. Note that it is fully endorsed by the medical profession.

2 •

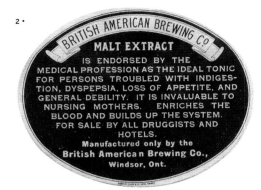

NEAR BEER AND PATENT MEDICINES

1 •

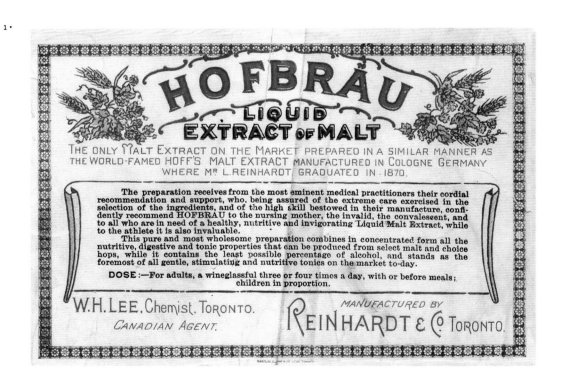

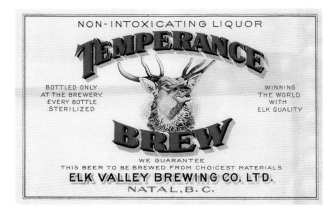

3 • "Wanna Beer," a so-called temperance beer sold by Rose and Laflamme Ltd., promised all the appearance and taste of the real thing but without the alcohol.

5 • "Temperance Brew," another low-alcohol beer, was produced by Elk Valley Brewing. Elk Valley was founded in southeastern British Columbia in 1908.

4 • Another "non-intoxicating" brew, this one was manufactured just before World War I by a Montreal brewer appealing to the enthusiasm for temperance.

Prohibition had its sceptics. Among them was Toronto's leading prewar intellectual, Goldwin Smith. In his speeches and articles Smith argued that while temperance was a sensible personal choice, complete prohibition was unnecessary and unenforceable. More than that, it was, he believed, a form of tyranny imposed by the government.

■ R.W. Scott, by whose name the Canada Temperance Act was better known, was a former Ottawa mayor and a member of the legislature from Canada West who originally supported the Conservative Party. Post-Confederation he switched to the Liberal camp and following the Pacific Scandal that drove John A. Macdonald from office late in 1873, Scott joined the cabinet of the new Liberal prime minister, Alexander Mackenzie. The following spring Mackenzie appointed Scott to the Senate where he served as Liberal leader for many years. He also filled in for various cabinet ministers while they were absent. Scott was a long-time teetotaller and the Canada Temperance Act, which he drafted, was his best-known legislative achievement. When Wilfrid Laurier became prime minister in 1896 Scott joined his cabinet as secretary of state. A vegetarian who believed in physical exercise, he remained vigorous until the end, speaking in the Senate for the last time just six weeks before his death in April 1913 at the age of eighty-four.

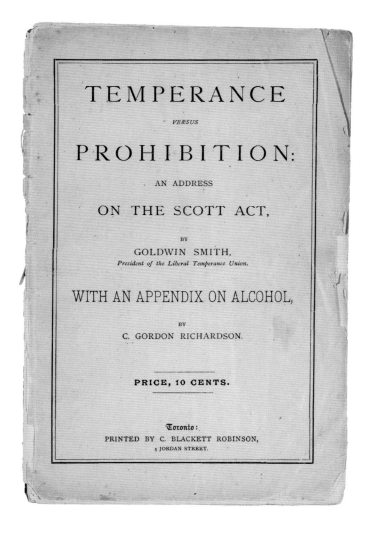

TEMPERANCE

VERSUS

PROHIBITION:

AN ADDRESS

ON THE SCOTT ACT,

BY

GOLDWIN SMITH,
President of the Liberal Temperance Union.

WITH AN APPENDIX ON ALCOHOL,

BY

C. GORDON RICHARDSON.

PRICE, 10 CENTS.

Toronto:
PRINTED BY C. BLACKETT ROBINSON,
5 JORDAN STREET.

impose their own liquor control. Residents voting in local plebiscites could decide to prohibit the sale of alcohol in their community. This approach seemed to be responsive to the wishes of the grassroots and allowed activists to work little by little to spread the dry message. It also allowed politicians to duck responsibility for the issue.

In 1878 the federal government passed the first piece of legislation aimed at controlling the consumption of liquor right across the country. The Canada Temperance Act, better known as the Scott Act after its sponsor, Secretary of State R.W. Scott, embodied the official position of Prime Minister Alexander Mackenzie and his Liberal Party, which was that outright prohibition imposed by the state was not advisable. "You cannot entirely control the drinking usages of society by prohibitory laws," Scott argued. "People must be educated to correct views on the subject before they can be kept sober. I should consider it a farce to pass a prohibitory law in [North] America at present or to prohibit the importation of liquor, because it could not be enforced." What Scott and his Liberal colleagues hoped to achieve with their law was a gradual transition to

temperance and to make full prohibition a possibility in communities where it could be shown that the people wanted it. Basically the Scott Act took the Dunkin Act, with its provisions for local option in Quebec and Ontario, and applied it in the rest of Canada. If one quarter of the electors in any city or county petitioned for a vote then a plebiscite would be held and if a majority of the votes were cast in favour of prohibition then the sale of liquor in that community would be banned, except for medical, religious or industrial uses.

The Maritime provinces jumped on the local option bandwagon. Following the lead of Fredericton, New Brunswick, the first place in Canada to use the new federal legislation to go dry, seven other Maritime communities almost immediately voted to ban the sale of alcohol. By the end of the century seventy percent of the region's population lived in areas that were at least nominally dry. Likewise in Ontario, twenty-five counties and two cities voted for local option. Out west, the North-West Territories between Manitoba and the Rockies, not yet organized into provinces, experimented with their own form of prohibition. Not only

THE SPEECH FROM THE THRONE.

THE WOMAN'S CHRISTIAN TEMPERANCE UNION

■ WOMEN PLAYED AN IMPOR- tant, if auxiliary, role in the early temperance movement in support of the male-led societies and lodges. During the 1870s a group of Ontario women activists, discouraged that the movement had so far failed to achieve a sober society, decided to take matters into their own hands. Late in 1874 Letitia Youmans, an intensely religious Sunday-school teacher from Picton, Ontario, organized a local chapter of the Woman's Christian Temperance Union (WCTU), an organization founded in the United States earlier that year.

Youmans was an impassioned speaker and an effective organizer. She set her sights on obtaining local option for her home county, Prince Edward County. Following a spirited campaign the county did vote to go dry by a majority of six hundred votes. But the victory was short-lived. Two years later, in 1877, Prince Edward County voted to repeal local option, a decision that left Youmans disappointed but not defeated. That same year the WCTU brought its Ontario chapters together in a province-wide organization with Youmans as the first president. Members took a pledge "to abstain from all distilled, fermented and malt liquors including beer, wine and cider as a beverage and to employ all proper means to discourage the use of and traffic in the same." When it expanded to become a national organization in 1883, again with Youmans as president, the WCTU was Canada's first non-denominational, nationwide women's group.

Temperance was its initiating cause but the Union soon took on a broad range of issues that seemed to affect the well-being of women, including the struggle to obtain the vote. For women like Youmans, alcohol was inseparable from poverty, crime and household abuse. The women of the WCTU sometimes faced ridicule, indifference, even violence, in response to their efforts. But they persevered, helping to achieve their objective of full prohibition during World War I.

The Loyal Temperance Legion was the children's branch of the Woman's Christian Temperance Union. Its motto was "Tremble, King Alcohol, We Shall Grow Up." Temperance activists believed in involving children in the cause from a young age.

was trading liquor with the First Nations illegal but so was the importation, sale and possession of alcoholic beverages of any kind by anyone, except by special permit issued by the lieutenant governor. Even with the arrival of the North West Mounted Police in 1874 it was obvious that such a law was unenforceable. The territory was too vast; the opportunities for skirting the law too tempting. The Mounties concentrated their efforts on eradicating the whisky trade with First Nations people while the rest of the population carried on as if prohibition did not exist. "Liquor is run into the country in every conceivable manner," reported the NWMP Commissioner, "in barrels of sugar, salt, and as ginger ale, and even in neatly constructed imitation eggs, and respectable people, who otherwise are honest, will resort to every device to evade the liquor laws…" Enforcing the law simply earned the Mounties the disrespect of the population. Not to mention that drinking was widespread among the police themselves.

In Manitoba and the eastern provinces, local option proved almost as ineffective as total prohibition was in the Territories. After the initial flush of enthusiasm, many of the counties that voted themselves dry took a second look and voted themselves wet again. During the 1880s most of the counties in Ontario rescinded local option and in Quebec the movement had not been as popular anyway. In practice it just did not prove all that effective since there was nothing to stop determined drinkers from bringing in alcohol from the next town over or from simply visiting a neighbouring "wet" community to get a drink. Officials had no appetite for enforcing the ban, and even if they had, the required police presence was not available. The Scott Act resulted in a sprinkling of dry islands in a vast sea of "wetness." For prohibitionists, it was no remedy for the evil that they believed was at work in Canada.

■ AS THE ENTHUSIASM FOR LOCAL OPTION waxed and waned in different parts of the country, prohibitionists recognized that the future of their movement lay not with local initiatives but with federal legislation, which would have to be forced on a reluctant government by a determined national effort. The roots of such a national movement were planted the year after Confederation when a group of activists met at the Temperance

In Western Canada, where prohibition was enforced by the North West Mounted Police, it was often the police themselves who violated the law. Here a pair of Mounties share a drink with a friend around a homemade still.

1 •   2 •   3 •   4 •

Temperance and prohibition were part of a larger movement for social reform in Canada in the nineteenth century. In the cities especially, campaigns to eradicate poverty, end disease, improve sanitation, and help neglected children all accompanied the growth of the industrial economy. Alcohol abuse was considered to be a significant contributor to all these social problems. Many people believed that closing the bar would do more than any other single thing to improve life for ordinary Canadians.

1 • The coat of arms of the Executive Council of the Canada Temperance Union, the founding of which was an important milestone in the formation of a national prohibition movement.

2 • The seal of the Chatham, Ontario, division of the Society of Temperance shows a convert to the cause smashing a liquor bottle and the sun rising on a new day.

3 • Seal of the Neal Dow Division of the Society of Temperance in Montreal. Dow was the mayor of Portland, Maine, and the sponsor of the 1851 "Maine Law" which was the model for later attempts to impose prohibition in Canada.

4 • Seal of the Woodville, Ontario, division of the Society shows a zealot taking an axe to a barrel of whisky.

Hall in Toronto and formed the Canada Temperance Union (CTU) to carry the struggle for "total abstinence" into the political arena. The following year the CTU shifted gears, deciding to confine its work to Ontario and renaming itself the Ontario Temperance and Prohibitory League. The plan was to form a comparable league in each province, then knit them together into a national organization. This ambition was partly realized in 1873 when a provincial league from Quebec joined with the one in Ontario to create the nucleus of a nationwide movement. Members lobbied the federal government insistently, bombarding Parliament with petitions asking for a prohibitory law. And Parliament was listening. In 1874 the Liberal government appointed a two-person commission to investigate how prohibition was being applied south of the border. A year later the commissioners submitted their report. While they did not come right out and endorse prohibition, they did provide a substantial body of information in its favour and based on the report the Canadian Senate passed a resolution affirming the need for a prohibitory law.

It was in this optimistic context that 285 delegates from Ontario, Quebec and the Maritime provinces gathered at the YMCA Auditorium in Montreal in mid-September 1875, to discuss the best way to achieve "nothing short of total prohibition." Brimming with enthusiasm, convinced that the longed-for goal was just around the corner, the convention voted to create a new national organization to keep up the pressure on the federal government. Out of this determination came the creation of the Dominion Alliance for the Total Suppression of the Liquor Traffic. In the years ahead it was the Alliance, with chapters in every province and thousands of activists enlisted in the cause, that would spearhead the struggle to eradicate the liquor traffic in Canada.

■   IN 1892 JOHN A. MACDONALD'S CONservative government, feeling the mounting pressure of public opinion, appointed a Royal Commission on the Liquor Traffic to study the feasibility of dry legislation. Prohibitionists would have been excused for thinking they stood at last on the brink of a great victory. Yet despite its apparent success, the movement was frustrated. The struggle had been going on for two generations, yet prohibition

This unique map shows the Temperance Railroad carrying passengers along its main line, the "Great Destruction Route," and its various feeder lines, past Rum Jug Lake and Mount Fear, through the State of Deceit and the State of Depravity to the State of Darkness. Every community and landmark on the map suggests the awful consequences of intemperance. It was hoped that copies of the map would be found in every home, hotel, school, church and railway station, encouraging sinners to climb aboard the Great Celestial Route.

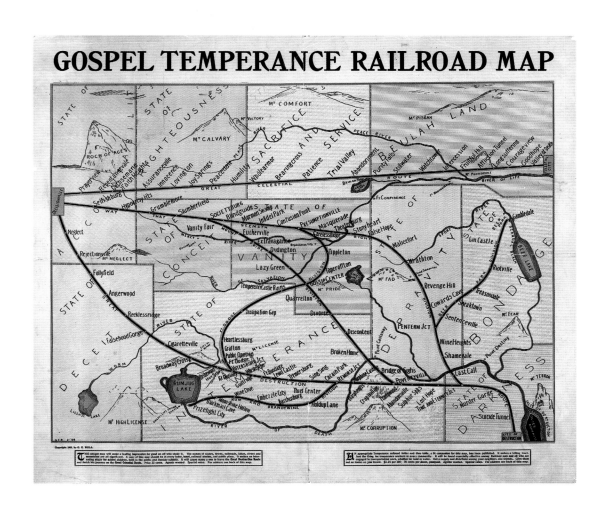

TEMPERANCE AND CHILDREN

■ TEMPERANCE ADVOCATES did not neglect children when it came to spreading the message of sobriety and abstinence. "Be sure and save the children, and the fathers and mothers will follow" was a guiding principle of the movement. Information about alcohol abuse was disseminated through the schools but the most effective strategy was to create separate organizations for the children themselves. The Cadets of Temperance, the Daughters of Temperance and the Cold Water Army were some of the youth groups that sprang up across the country, but the most popular were the Bands of Hope.

The Bands originated in England in 1847, then migrated to British North America. Based on a Sunday-school model, they were nonetheless non-denominational and came to be associated most prominently with the Woman's Christian Temperance Union. Activities included concerts, parades, and lectures about the evils of alcohol.

Every child took the pledge to abstain from alcohol and learned to sing temperance songs, a sample of which went:

> Touch not the foaming,
> tempting glass,
> Nor look upon the wine!
> A serpent vile is hid within
> The liquid of the vine.

By 1890 close to fifteen thousand children in Ontario alone were members of a Band of Hope.

According to his membership card, young Samuel Rogers joined a Band of Hope in July 1886. As a member he took the pledge "to abstain from all intoxicating drinks" and attended lectures and other activities designed to instill a distaste for alcohol.

was still an aspiration, not a reality. The local option approach was not working. The courts were still undecided about which level of government had the constitutional jurisdiction to actually "banish the bar." Even the Royal Commission was seen as a device for delaying or sabotaging prohibition, instead of moving it along. The hearings would provide an opportunity for the liquor proponents to spread their self-interested lies, prohibitionists argued, and the government would be given an excuse to ignore the movement. Paradoxically, organizations like the Dominion Alliance for the Total Suppression of the Liquor Traffic saw the Royal Commission as a defeat, not a victory.

There is little question that the Royal Commission on the Liquor Traffic was the stacked deck that the Alliance said it was. Four of the five commissioners opposed prohibition. From the beginning, there was little chance that they were going to change their minds and report in its favour. Nonetheless the Alliance believed it had to participate in the hearings if only to ensure that someone was on hand to present the other side. As the Commission made its way across Canada during 1892 and the early

part of 1893, listening to the testimony of a variety of public officials, the secretary of the Alliance, Frank Spence, attended most of the meetings.

In March 1895 the federal government released the final report of the Royal Commission, all seven volumes and 5,870 pages of it. As Spence and his colleagues had expected, it shied away from endorsing the idea of prohibition. The report documented the extent of alcohol consumption in the country and also the significant economic contribution of the brewing and distilling industries, in terms of jobs, capital investment and not least, several million dollars that the different levels of government annually collected in the form of licence fees, customs duties and excise taxes. The majority report, endorsed by four of the five commissioners, proposed limited reforms to bar licensing and hours of service but refused to accept that a total liquor ban was necessary or feasible. The federal government had what it wanted: an excuse to do nothing.

■ WHILE THE FEDERAL GOVERNMENT waited on the results of the Royal Commission, the Dominion Alliance and its allies

The Loyal Temperance Legion, the children's wing of the WCTU, focused its efforts on children ages six to twelve. The aim was to promote abstinence from alcohol and tobacco. Members were awarded pins and badges like these to show their dedication to the cause.

Sometimes prohibition was enforced by employers rather than governments. Sewell Moody was a pioneer lumberman in British Columbia and owner of a sawmill on the north shore of Burrard Inlet from 1865 to 1875. The community that grew up around the mill was called Moodyville, the beginning of North Vancouver. Moody was a teetotaller and forbade the consumption of alcohol in his town. He drowned when a ship in which he was travelling to San Francisco went down off Cape Flattery in 1875. Following his death, life at Moodyville loosened up a bit, judging by the fact that the local hotel was selling spirits a few years later. This green glass gin bottle was discovered in the community's former dump in 1972 but it has been dated to the late 1880s. Its four-sided shape was designed to fit in a case of a dozen bottles. Gin, a working man's drink, was imported from Holland, where Rotterdam alone had three hundred distilleries.

continued to besiege the provincial governments with their demands for prohibitory laws. In response, between 1892 and 1894 all of the English-language provinces (remembering that Alberta and Saskatchewan did not yet have provincial status and Newfoundland did not join Confederation for another half century) took steps to consult popular opinion on the issue. In four provinces the electorate expressed their views in plebiscites; New Brunswick made do with a legislative resolution. The plebiscites began in July 1892 in Manitoba and concluded in mid-March 1894 in Nova Scotia. In every province voters opted overwhelmingly to go dry. Yet despite this apparent tidal wave of popular support, no province took the next step and introduced prohibition. For one thing, voter turnout for the plebiscites had been low, which gave the politicians an excuse to go slow. Second, the issue of constitutional jurisdiction was still hung up in the courts. It was pointless to legislate prohibition, politicians argued, if the law would simply be overturned. Ontario Premier Oliver Mowat appeared to go the furthest to mollify prohibitionist forces. Addressing a delegation of activists just a month after the plebiscite, he

promised that if the court ruled that a province could ban the sale of liquor then he would do so. And if the court ruled that a province had only partial jurisdiction, then "I will introduce such a prohibitory bill as the decision will warrant." In spite of all their experience with the fickleness of politicians, the prohibitionists accepted this declaration as an ironclad guarantee and left their meeting with the Premier full of optimism.

On May 9, 1896, the Judicial Committee of the Privy Council in England – then the court of final appeal on Canadian legal matters – finally handed down its ruling. Provinces, the committee ruled, had the constitutional authority to control the sale of alcoholic beverages within their borders, though only the federal government could ban its manufacture and importation. Qualified good news, apparently, for the forces of prohibition which in Ontario at least expected the government to make good on Oliver Mowat's promise to ban the bar. But Mowat had gone on to his higher reward – that is, a job in the federal cabinet and a seat in the Senate – and his successor as premier, Arthur Hardy, was not committed to the same

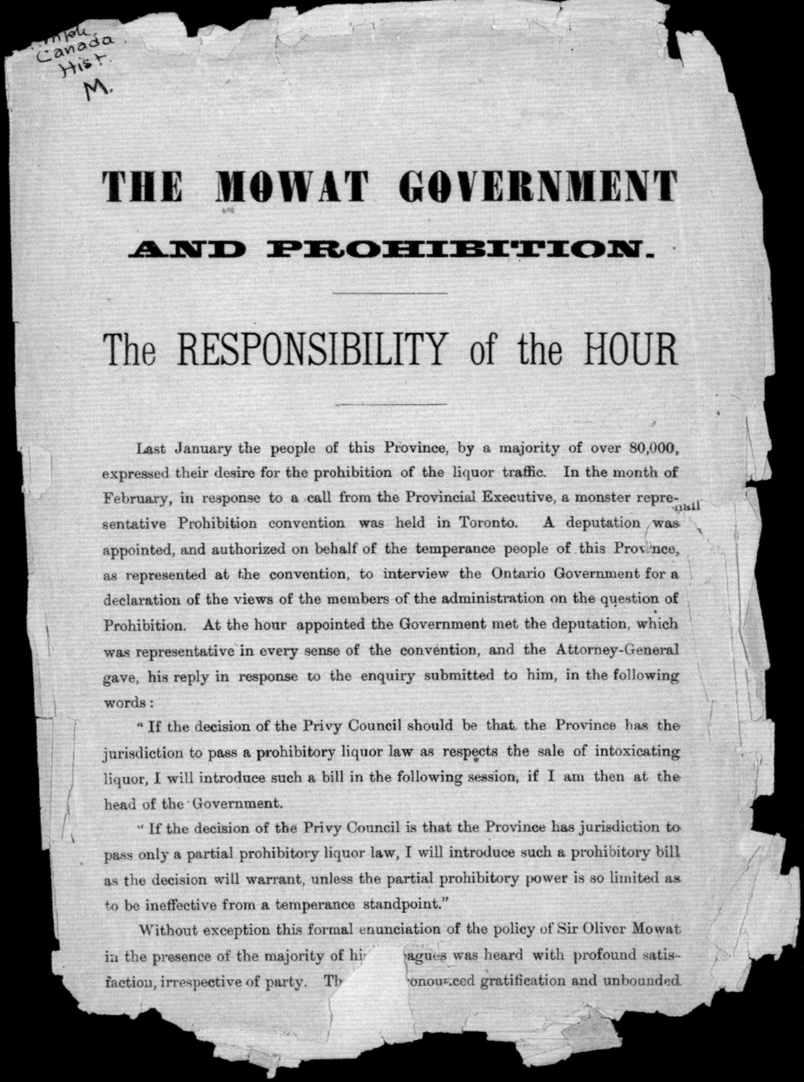

THE MOWAT GOVERNMENT
AND PROHIBITION.

The RESPONSIBILITY of the HOUR

Last January the people of this Province, by a majority of over 80,000, expressed their desire for the prohibition of the liquor traffic. In the month of February, in response to a call from the Provincial Executive, a monster representative Prohibition convention was held in Toronto. A deputation was appointed, and authorized on behalf of the temperance people of this Province, as represented at the convention, to interview the Ontario Government for a declaration of the views of the members of the administration on the question of Prohibition. At the hour appointed the Government met the deputation, which was representative in every sense of the convention, and the Attorney-General gave, his reply in response to the enquiry submitted to him, in the following words :

" If the decision of the Privy Council should be that the Province has the jurisdiction to pass a prohibitory liquor law as respects the sale of intoxicating liquor, I will introduce such a bill in the following session, if I am then at the head of the Government.

" If the decision of the Privy Council is that the Province has jurisdiction to pass only a partial prohibitory liquor law, I will introduce such a prohibitory bill as the decision will warrant, unless the partial prohibitory power is so limited as to be ineffective from a temperance standpoint."

Without exception this formal enunciation of the policy of Sir Oliver Mowat in the presence of the majority of his [c]olleagues was heard with profound satisfaction, irrespective of party. The [p]ronounced gratification and unbounded

On the first day of January 1894, the people of Ontario voted in a plebiscite by a majority of more than eighty-one thousand to introduce prohibition. Still, Premier Oliver Mowat refused to act, claiming that it was not clear whether the province had the constitutional authority. He promised to bring in a liquor ban if the court ruled that he could. But by the time the highest court did just that, Mowat had left office and his successor as premier, Arthur Hardy, did not feel bound by any promise. Prohibition activists felt betrayed and struck back with a propaganda campaign against the government, of which this pamphlet was a part. But Hardy remained unmoved. And he was not alone. Despite plebiscite after plebiscite in favour of prohibition, politicians in almost every province were reluctant to impose it.

■ JOHN WILSON BENGOUGH was Canada's pre-eminent political cartoonist of the late nineteenth century. He was born in Toronto in 1851 and there he launched the satiric magazine *Grip* when he was just twenty-two years old. For twenty years *Grip* mocked the pretensions and policies of leading politicians from the perspective of a committed social reformer. Its operating principle was that "The Pun is mightier than the Sword." Prohibition was one of Bengough's favourite causes. He opposed alcohol because he thought it was particularly destructive of the working class. But he was not a single-issue reformer. Among his many other causes were women's suffrage and the single tax (a radical taxation system proposed by the American social theorist Henry George).

After *Grip* folded during the economic recession of the early 1890s, Bengough continued to publish his caricatures in a variety of publications. He also gave highly popular public lectures – his so-called "chalk talks" – on social reform issues. Not content to criticize from the sidelines, Bengough served three terms as alderman in his native city. During World War I he used his talents in support of the war effort and conscription. Active to the end, he died at home in 1923 at the age of seventy-two, working on a cartoon.

John Wilson Bengough, an outspoken supporter of prohibition, published this "book of fables" in 1897. The book contained a series of brief, illustrated stories, each one ending with a moral, such as "the licensed liquor traffic slays thousands every year," or "the liquor traffic is a parasite upon legitimate business."

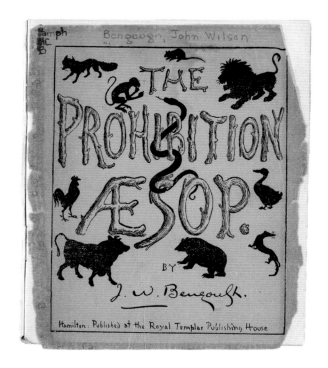

This button celebrates the victory of Wilfrid Laurier and his Liberal Party in the national election of 1896. The Liberals had promised to hold a country-wide referendum on the question of prohibition and they carried out this promise on September 29, 1898. The country voted Yes by a slim majority, but Laurier decided No. The button was made by Whitehead & Hoag, a New Jersey novelties company that first patented the celluloid button in the 1890s. This marks the first time such buttons were used in a Canadian election.

policy. Hardy's government introduced a liquor bill that stopped well short of full prohibition. When the Alliance reacted with outrage at what it saw to be a breach of faith, Hardy insisted that the experience of the past few years had shown the effectiveness of the gradualist approach. Ontario, he said, was not ready for a total alcohol ban – despite the results of the provincial plebiscite, apparently – and the government was not prepared to get out ahead of public opinion on the issue.

But as so often happened when it came to prohibition, as one door closed another opened. In June 1893 the federal Liberal Party had held a convention in Ottawa, the first national political party convention in the country's history. It turned out to be an event that would energize the party and its leader Wilfrid Laurier, and propel them to an election victory three years later. Frank Spence was among the 1,800 party faithful in attendance, working the backrooms in an attempt to get a prohibition plank added to the platform. While his fellow Liberals were not prepared to go that far, they were prepared to approve a resolution promising that, if elected, a Laurier government would put the question to a national vote. Which

is exactly what happened. On June 23, 1896, voters elected the Laurier Liberals with a clear majority. Canadians had their first francophone prime minister and prohibitionists had reason to hope. Laurier personally was no teetotaller, and he knew that the issue was potentially divisive, pitting his home province of Quebec, where dry support was weak, against the rest of the country. Nonetheless, he had promised to honour the party platform and in August 1898 the government announced that a plebiscite would occur on September 29 asking the question: "Are you in favour of passing an Act prohibiting the importation, manufacture, or sale of spirits, wine, ale, cider, and all other alcoholic liquors for use as a beverage?" It would be the first national plebiscite ever held in Canada on any subject. (The terms "plebiscite" and "referendum" were used interchangeably but are technically different things: the result of a referendum is considered binding on the government while a plebiscite is merely advisory and does not necessarily require the government to act.)

When the ballots were counted, the results showed that 278,380 Canadians favoured a prohibition law, a majority of

51 percent of the votes cast. The Yes side had won. But a majority of one percent was never going to be enough to force the government's hand. For one thing, voter turnout was low, only 44 percent, compared to a 63 percent turnout in the most recent federal election. As well, one province, Quebec, had voted decisively against the proposition. It was unrealistic to expect Laurier to proceed against the wishes of the French-speaking population. That said, the issue of French-English divisiveness should not be exaggerated. There was significant opposition to prohibition outside Quebec as well. In Ontario, 42 percent voted No; in British Columbia, 45 percent. The Alliance was not accurate when it called the "anti" vote a "French vote." If anything, the result showed that the plebiscite, because it relied on voter turnout, was an inexact tool for measuring public opinion.

The outcome of the national vote in 1898 by no means brought an end to the efforts of the Dominion Alliance or to the plebiscite movement. The Alliance launched the "100,000 Voters Movement," a campaign to convince that many electors to pledge not to support any candidate who did not support

In Manitoba in 1902 the provincial government held yet another plebiscite and some prohibitionists, angry at what they saw to be a delaying tactic, urged voters not to participate. The local chapter of the Dominion Alliance fractured and prohibition went down to defeat.

■ One of the most energetic campaigners in favour of prohibition was the author and activist Nellie McClung. More famous today as a leader of the struggle for women's suffrage, a political movement that advanced hand in hand with prohibition, McClung was a stalwart member of the Woman's Christian Temperance Union. During the wartime plebiscites in Western Canada she marched, demonstrated, harangued and debated in favour of prohibition. One of the reasons McClung and other suffragists fought so hard for the vote was so that an aroused female electorate could ban the liquor trade.

A prolific writer, McClung published her first novel, *Sowing Seeds in Danny*, in 1908. It became a national bestseller and launched her career as a public speaker. In all she published sixteen books: novels, essays, stories and poems. Married with five children, she and her husband, a druggist and business executive, moved from Winnipeg to Edmonton in 1915. During the 1920s she served a five-year term in the Alberta legislature and was one of the five activists (the "Famous 5") who fought to have women recognized as "persons" by the law. In 1932 the McClungs moved to Vancouver Island. She died in 1951.

Pampl. Social. II

Dominion Alliance for the Total Suppression of the Liquor Traffic. Manitoba Branch

Dominion Alliance Manifesto

Also Citizens' Reasons for Ignoring the So-Called Referendum

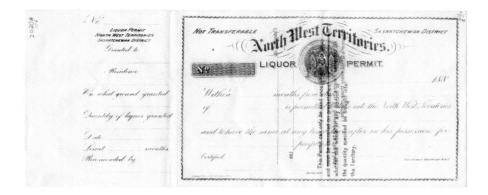

prohibition. The objective was to fill the House of Commons with prohibitionists, no matter what their party affiliation or their positions on other issues. At the same time two more provincial votes took place, both in 1902. In Manitoba, a divided prohibition movement went down to defeat, while in Ontario voters approved a ban by 65.8 percent to 34.2 percent only to be told by the government once again that the turnout was not large enough to justify taking action.

There was one exception to the repeated failure of the movement to win government approval. In 1900 the legislature of Prince Edward Island passed a prohibition law, which came into effect gradually as a majority of the voters in each of the counties agreed to repeal the federal Scott Act. By 1906 this had been done and the sale of liquor became illegal across the Island except in special circumstances. The liquor ban gave rise to the usual circumventions. Smugglers ferried in booze from out of province, moonshiners peddled their own homebrew, druggists and doctors over-prescribed the use of alcohol for spurious medical reasons. But the law remained on the books, with amendments, until 1948 and PEI had the distinction of

being the first province to go dry.

■ ALONG WITH WOMEN'S SUFFRAGE, there was no more contentious topic than prohibition in Victorian Canada. Not surprisingly, almost everyone had something to say about it. Some of the leading intellectuals and journalists in the country mounted the public platform to refute the arguments of the prohibitionists. In Ontario, Goldwin Smith identified himself with the "wet" cause. Smith had emigrated to the United States from his native England in 1868, then moved north to Canada three years later. He had been a professor of history both at Oxford University and in New York, but in Toronto he married a wealthy widow and settled into a new life as man of letters and public provocateur. He wrote extensively for the leading newspapers and magazines, his essays often appearing above a nom de plume, The Bystander. "Annexation" Smith was best known for his advocacy of union with the United States. He was an Anglo-Saxon supremacist who believed that the American Revolution had been a disaster because it sundered the unity of the English-speaking people of the New World. Canadian nationality

In the North-West Territories (today's Alberta and Saskatchewan) alcoholic beverages were legal only by obtaining a special liquor permit signed by the lieutenant governor. This blank permit from the Saskatchewan District dates from the 1880s.

BELOW A whisky bottle from Montreal dating to the 1890s. There were not yet any government liquor stores; alcohol was purchased at general stores and grocery stores. The label indicates this brand was "whisky blanc" or "white whisky," a type of unaged or lightly aged whisky that resembled gin more than conventional Scotch or rye.

RIGHT For some the bar was a good place to relax with friends. To others it was a den of iniquity where working men squandered their pay and women fell into depravity. The bar in the Alberta Hotel in Crossfield, north of Calgary, was a typical small-town watering hole when this photograph was taken c. 1910.

The prohibition movement was sometimes criticized for snobbery and a bias against the working class since it was invariably working people who were accused of squandering their wages in the bar and destroying their families by drunkenness. Here members of a work crew on the Temiskaming and Northern Ontario Railway seem to be enjoying a relaxing drink at their work camp at Englehart, Ontario, in 1908.

was, in his view, "a lost cause," not least because of the presence of the Québécois, whom he considered a backward, priest-ridden community. Better to drown the French in a continental union of English-speaking people. "The two portions of the Anglo-Saxon race on this continent are one people," he insisted.

Smith was what today is called a public intellectual. He was not reticent about expressing his views – on the platform and in the press – on a wide range of public issues. He was a great opposer, and among the things he opposed was prohibition. "Temperance means moderate use," he asserted; "Prohibition means total and enforced abstinence. Temperance, as I believe, is rational, practicable, and commended by the Gospel, while enforced abstinence is not." The proper question, he argued, was not whether excessive drinking was a bad thing – he agreed it was "a beastly and degrading vice" – but whether trying to control it through prohibition did more harm than good. Smith believed that most of the claims that prohibitionists made about the evils of alcohol were overblown. It was not a poison, he said; people had been enjoying it in moderation

for centuries. Nor was it the cause of as much crime and disease as the most extreme advocates of prohibition claimed. Moreover, experience showed that wherever a total ban was implemented the results were disastrous. The law could not be enforced and attempts to do so encouraged furtive consumption, suspicion and ill will between neighbours and in the end actually increased drunkenness. Prohibition replaced a regulated liquor trade with an illicit one "by worse men in worse places." And lastly, it deprived the government of tax revenue as money that might have gone to public services was spent on contraband trade.

That prohibition was a form of tyranny was also the view of another outspoken "wet," Stephen Leacock. Known today principally as a humorous writer, Leacock was a trained political economist and for many years a member of the department of economics and political science at Montreal's McGill University. But he never liked academia much, preferring to address a broader audience on topical public issues. Government leaders sought him out for advice and his essays appeared in all the leading publications. In 1919 he summed up his views on the

liquor question in an article titled "The Tyranny of Prohibition." Like Goldwin Smith, Leacock was an unapologetic social drinker who resented that a harmless indulgence might be made illegal by people he considered religious fanatics. In his view, if you didn't want to drink, you shouldn't, but you ought not to turn someone who did drink into a criminal. "There is no more reason why you should put a criminal penalty upon the use of beer than you should on the use of cucumbers."

Leacock believed that the success of the prohibition movement revealed a weakness in parliamentary democracy. Because politicians only cared about getting elected, they were susceptible to the views of a "relentless and fanatical minority" who simply made more noise than the majority of voters who were either intimidated or uninterested. Leacock's contempt for the politicians who were failing to stand up to the "new tyranny" ran deep. "The ordinary politician," he wrote, "is merely busy picking up his votes from the mud of democracy like the ramasseur of the Parisian streets picking up cigar butts." As he explained it, prohibition was coming about insidiously, community by community,

"Have You Any Boys?" asks this leaflet from the 1898 national referendum campaign, urging people to vote in favour of prohibition. The leaflet claims that five thousand individuals died in Canada every year "as a result of the Liquor Traffic" and suggested that families were losing that many young men "to keep up the supply." Canadians voted in favour but the government chose not to introduce prohibition, arguing the result was inconclusive.

Have You Any Boys?

At a meeting of the Ohio Liquor League a short time since one of the officers gave the following bit of advice to the members. It is quite in keeping with the diabolical nature of the business:

"It will appear from these facts, gentlemen, that the success of our business is dependent largely upon the creation of appetite for drink. Men who drink liquor, like others, will die, and if there is no new appetite created, our counters will be empty as will be our coffers. Our children will go hungry or we must change our business to that of some other more remunerative. The open field for the creation of this appetite is among the boys. After men have grown and their habits are formed, they rarely ever change in this regard. It will be needful therefore that this missionary work be done among the boys, and I make the suggestion, gentlemen, that nickles expended in treats now, will return in dollars to your tills after the appetite has been formed. Above all things create appetite."

HOW DOES THAT STRIKE YOU?

5000 PERSONS die off in Canada every year as the result of the Liquor Traffic. 5000 Boys are needed to keep up the supply. Have you any boys to spare for the purpose? As long as the traffic exists, they must be furnished. If you do not contribute, some other family must give more than its share. Is that fair?

If you think it is about time for this sort of thing to stop, mark your ballot thus:

| Are you in favor of passing an act prohibiting the importation, manufacture or sale of spirits, wine, ale, beer, cider and all other alcoholic liquors for use as beverages? | YES. X | NO. |

Remember September 29.
Down with the Liquor Traffic!

■ Bob Edwards, who was born in Scotland, came to Alberta when he was thirty-seven years old after kicking around the United States for several years. He published a number of newspapers, most notably the satiric Calgary weekly, the *Eye Opener* (1903–09, 1911–22). The paper gained a national audience for its wit and its scathing political commentary. Edwards was a notorious tippler who made no secret of his love for the barroom. ("I am a prohibitionist," he once wrote. "What I propose to prohibit is the reckless use of water.") But he was also a maverick, and during the war he reconsidered his position. Alberta held a prohibition plebiscite in 1916 and Edwards urged voters to support it, in part because of the dreadful effects of excessive drinking on family stability. However, once the law was in place and he saw how it led to moonshining and bootlegging, he turned around and urged its repeal. Despite the fact that Edwards made a career out of lampooning politicians, in the end he became one, winning election to the Alberta legislature as an independent in 1921. When he died in November 1922 after making just one speech, he was buried with a pocket flask of whisky.

OPPOSITE Canadian children were enlisted as soldiers in the war on the liquor traffic, following the example of these British youngsters marching in the streets of London in 1917 in support of prohibition. During the war, it was argued, valuable resources should not be wasted on the manufacture of alcohol.

RIGHT A group of Sunday-school children in Calgary joins the prohibition campaign during the 1915 Alberta plebiscite. The main Protestant churches – Presbyterian, Methodist, Baptist – worked tirelessly to "close the saloon." Their efforts paid off as Alberta voters opted solidly for prohibition, which was introduced provincially on July 1, 1916.

plebiscite by plebiscite. Most people did not complain because if their community went dry they could always bring in their alcohol from outside. "They did not realize," he warned, "that the time was coming when there would be no outside"; that they would wake up one day to discover the whole country in thrall to the minority.

In British Columbia, another prominent "wet" made the argument that prohibition would turn Canadians into emasculated, cultural weaklings. Appearing before the Royal Commission on the Liquor Traffic in November 1892, the province's chief justice, Sir Matthew Begbie, made the argument that the use of alcohol in moderation was a sign not just of social superiority but of cultural superiority as well. Only members of "inferior races" practised prohibition, he said, because they didn't know how to handle their liquor. Begbie was talking here about the Chinese and the "Hindoos" (i.e. South Asians) whose arrival in British Columbia at this time was causing anxiety among the Anglo-Canadian majority. Their supposed distaste for liquor was, according to Begbie, another reason why these newcomers could not assimilate to the host culture. "I should

consider it a mark of inferiority if a man cannot drink, or does not drink, and if he will not drink," he told the commissioners. "I would be sorry to see men, white men, reduced to the level of Hindoos…"

Both sides of the liquor debate pushed logic to the extremes when making the case for and against prohibition. For the most fervent advocates of the dry side, alcohol was responsible for every evil that afflicted modern society: divorce, poverty, child and spousal abuse, murder and mental illness. For some of the wets, prohibition was, in the words of Stephen Leacock, "the worst, most dangerous and most subversive thing that has come upon us in half a century." It was a tyranny imposed on the majority by a fanatical minority and even, in Judge Begbie's view, a threat to the racial superiority of Anglo-Saxon civilization. Pretty clearly, for both sides the stakes were high.

■ DESPITE ALL THE CAMPAIGNS, PETI-tions, plebiscites and local option votes, it took a world war to make prohibition in Canada a reality. On August 4, 1914, the peaceful dog days of summer were shattered

by the outbreak of war between Germany and Britain. There was no question that Canada would join in on the side of the Mother Country. As Prime Minister Robert Borden told the House of Commons, "all are agreed, we stand shoulder to shoulder with Britain and the other British dominions in this quarrel." Canadians greeted the war with enthusiasm as an opportunity to strike a blow for freedom and civilization against German despotism. Young men hurried to enlist for fear that the victory would be won before they could get a taste of the action. By the spring of 1915, however, the true nature of the conflict became apparent as the armies got bogged down in a terrible stalemate. Canadians came to realize that the war was going to demand unprecedented suffering and sacrifice, on the battlefield and at home. In this context of national crisis and determination, prohibition got its second wind.

"Without the war," observed Stephen Leacock, "national prohibition would never have been voted…" The war added a number of seemingly compelling arguments to the prohibitionist cause. For one thing, young soldiers, many of them away from

After years of campaigning, and dozens of plebiscites, it was World War I that finally swung the pendulum in favour of prohibition. In 1918 the Unionist government led by Prime Minister Robert Borden imposed a nationwide ban on alcoholic beverages.

In this new atmosphere of national crisis, prohibition was seen as yet another sacrifice Canadians were expected to make to ensure victory in the armed struggle. As these posters indicate, everyone was being asked to contribute to the war effort, including, in this case, teenage boys. They were urged to become "Soldiers of the Soil" and take over farm work previously done by their fathers and elder brothers who had gone overseas to fight. The imagery equates service on the home front to military service. In the same way, Canadians were asked to give up alcohol in service of the greater good.

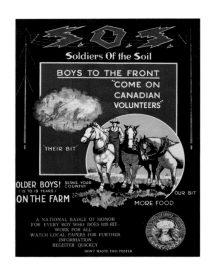

Even young children were drafted into the war effort on the home front. This poster from the Canada Food Board urged Canadians to grow their own vegetables so that produce from the farms could be sent overseas to feed the troops. Likewise, prohibition would make it possible to divert supplies of grain and sugar to maintain the military.

home for the first time, had to be protected from the sinful temptations that awaited them in Europe: cheap alcohol, prostitutes and venereal disease. Drunkenness would debilitate "our boys," weaken their resolve and leave them useless for fighting. And it wasn't just the soldiers who had to stay in fighting trim. The war situation challenged civilians as well to create a purified society that stood as a moral example to the depraved enemy. In the new spirit of sacrifice, drink seemed like a small thing to give up when others were called upon to give up so much. The home front was totally mobilized for the war effort. All resources were channelled toward supporting the armed forces overseas. Families started Victory Gardens to grow their own produce so as to make more food available for the troops. Children gathered scrap metal for munitions; fuel was rationed; industry re-engineered to produce war material instead of consumer goods. Scarce supplies of sugar and grain, the prohibitionists argued, could not be used to produce alcohol when they were needed to fight the Kaiser.

The war also sanctioned a new level of state interference in individual lives. The government introduced rationing of some items. Canadians tolerated widespread censorship of the news media; the country's chief press censor was even allowed to open the mail and listen to telephone calls. In 1917 Ottawa introduced the first income tax as a way to finance its contribution to the war, which by this time was costing almost a million dollars a day. Democracy itself was suspended as the government ruled by order-in-council under the terms of the emergency War Measures Act. The argument that prohibition represented an infringement of individual liberty lost much of its force when personal freedoms were expected to take a back seat to national security.

There was also an element of nativism to the prohibitionist propaganda during the war. Prior to 1914, hundreds of thousands of immigrants had come to Canada, many from Europe. Generally speaking, these newcomers were not sympathetic to abstinence. Once the war broke out, people who had come to Canada from what were now hostile countries – Germans, Turks, Bulgarians, Austrians, Hungarians – were transformed into "enemy aliens." Anglo-Canadians began to rethink their tolerant attitude

Beverage manufacturers recognized which way public sentiment was moving and attempted to identify themselves with the war effort. The medals on this label refer to the gold medal won by Labatt's India Pale Ale at the Paris Exposition of 1878.

■ During World War I, every province passed legislation prohibiting the sale of alcohol, except for Prince Edward Island which had already gone dry in 1906. These are the dates when prohibition went into effect:

Manitoba • June 1, 1916
Nova Scotia • June 30, 1916
Alberta • July 1, 1916
Ontario • September 17, 1916
New Brunswick • May 1, 1917
Saskatchewan • May 1, 1917
British Columbia • October 1, 1917
Yukon • May 1, 1918

Quebec passed a law banning the sale of alcohol as of May 1, 1919, but following a plebiscite endorsing the sale of beer, wine and cider the ban only applied to spirits.

toward the newcomers. As fear and suspicion spread, the newcomers' opposition to prohibition became one more reason to suspect their loyalty.

The bottom line was that the prohibition movement successfully linked itself to patriotism at a time when patriotism trumped all other values. Unless you supported a ban on drink, you were supporting the enemy. How could anyone defend the bar when Canadians were making necessary sacrifices in so many other areas? Sensing the urgency of this new consensus, provincial politicians lost little time in putting the matter to a vote. A series of plebiscites or referenda took place in Manitoba, Saskatchewan, Alberta and British Columbia, all of which led to provincial laws introducing prohibition. Ontario, Nova Scotia and New Brunswick introduced a ban without going to the trouble of holding a popular vote. (Only Quebec held back. Its legislature voted to ban retail sales of all alcoholic beverages beginning on May 1, 1919, but before the deadline rolled around a plebiscite revealed a majority of voters were in favour of keeping beer and wine legal so when the ban came it only involved spirits.)

■ THERE REMAINED ONE HOLDOUT FROM this surge to national prohibition: the federal government. The courts had ruled that Ottawa had sole jurisdiction over the manufacture and importation of alcoholic beverages. Even as the provinces shuttered their stores and turned off the beer taps, it was still possible for consumers to import liquor from outside producers. As a result, brewers and distillers could still make their product and distributors could still transport it from one province to another (and, of course, doctors could still prescribe it for medical reasons, a loophole that was widely exploited in all the provinces). The federal government seemed to represent the last hurdle before the finish line and the prohibitionists reintensified their efforts to convince Ottawa to join in.

In the autumn of 1917 Prime Minister Robert Borden, determined to form a united front to pursue the rest of the war, invited the opposition Liberals to join his Conservatives in a Union government. Opposition leader Wilfrid Laurier refused, but many of his English-speaking Liberals agreed to join Borden's coalition. In mid-December a national election gave the Unionists a solid

BELOW **Barkeepers in a line half a mile long hold up a banner protesting the introduction of prohibition at a parade in Toronto in March 1916.**

RIGHT **Prohibitionists gather signatures on a petition sponsored by the Committee of One Hundred during the same 1916 parade. Later that year the provincial government passed the Ontario Temperance Act, in large part due to the pressure exerted by the Committee's campaign.**

ONE WHO IS PLEASED

LAURIER POLICY MANIFESTO

THE KAISER:- "HOCH DER LAURIER POLICY ! IF HE WINS THERE WILL BE NO MORE CANADIANS TO WORRY ME" VOTE · UNION · GOVERNMENT

victory and almost immediately Borden announced that his government would be banning the importation of "intoxicating liquors," along with their transportation into any part of the Dominion where the sale was already illegal. As well, the manufacture of beverage alcohol would be stopped. All these measures would remain in force for a year following the arrival of peace (as it turned out, the end of 1919). "It is essential, and indeed vital, for the efficient conduct of the war," said Borden in making the announcement, "that wasteful or unnecessary expenditure should be prohibited, and that all articles capable of being utilized as food should be conserved. It is beyond question that the use of liquor affects adversely the realization of this purpose."

Once the orders-in-council implementing these restrictions came into effect on April 1, 1918, Canada came as close to total prohibition as it ever would in its history. In a year and a half the United States would follow suit, introducing the amendment to its Constitution that would inaugurate a thirteen-year period of prohibition south of the border. With the entire continent under some sort of ban on alcohol, the stage was set for one of the oddest, most contentious and most violent experiments in social control that North Americans have ever seen.

This seventeenth-century scene by the Spanish artist Diego Velazquez (1599-1660) is titled "The Triumph of Bacchus." Also known as "The Drinkers," it depicts the god of wine sharing a drink with a group of working men and captures a positive image of alcohol as a relief from the tribulations and mundanity of everyday life. In this sense the painting presents a counter-narrative to the fire and brimstone of the temperance/prohibition movement. Of course, temperance advocates might say that the painting portrays exactly the sort of overindulgence against which they were fighting.

Velazquez was the favourite painter of King Phillip IV, a great patron of the arts, who ruled Spain from 1621 until his death in 1665.

CHAPTER THREE

I am a bootlegger. I am not ashamed to admit it.
And a bootlegger I shall remain.

– ROCCO PERRI, Hamilton gangster

RUNNING THE BORDER

■ AROUND THE COAL-MINING TOWNS OF the Crowsnest Pass, Emilio Picariello was a cross between Robin Hood and the outlaw Clyde Barrow. Known as "Emperor Pic," he ran a handful of businesses, some of them legitimate, some less so. A heavy-set, dark-haired man with a luxurious black moustache, Picariello was an ebullient back-slapper much admired by his fellow Italian immigrants for his generosity to their community. When times were bad – and they often were in coal country – the Emperor distributed food hampers to the worst off. He donated to local charities, screened free moving-picture shows for the kids, and during the war reportedly bought $50,000 worth of Victory bonds to support the cause. He was also the biggest liquor smuggler in southern Alberta.

Picariello, who was born in Sicily in 1875, came to Canada around the turn of the century, settling in Toronto where he opened a store, married and began raising a family. In 1911 the Picariellos moved west to Fernie, British Columbia, where Emilio found work at a factory that produced pasta. Before long he was managing the plant and branching out into ice-cream making and a wine-importing business. He also developed a sideline selling used bottles to the local breweries, advertising himself as the "Bottle King." With the arrival of prohibition in Alberta on July 1, 1916, Picariello began exporting wine from his warehouse in Fernie to customers across the provincial border, an operation that was perfectly legal, at least for a time. The business went well and early in 1918 he purchased a hotel in Blairmore, Alberta, where he moved his family. Three months later, when the provincial government extended prohibition to include a ban on interprovincial liquor shipments, Picariello launched his career as a smuggler.

The Crowsnest was one of Canada's most productive coal-mining areas. After the Canadian Pacific had opened a southern rail line through the pass in 1898, mines had opened at several locations to provide the fuel that ran the trains. Mine owners imported a mostly immigrant labour force to do

LEFT In most pioneer settlements, liquor stores and saloons were among the first business established. This sturdy log cabin was home to the Edd and Joe Q.T. Saloon in Donald, BC, along the Canadian Pacific main line.

BELOW A travelling bootlegger displays his wares for the camera near Kelowna, BC, c. 1920. Note the shotgun, presumably brought along to guard against hijackers.

Emilio Picariello, every inch the respectable businessman, poses with his family in 1915. Picariello, one of the most active whisky runners in southwestern Alberta, hanged for the murder of a provincial police officer in 1923.

the hard, dangerous work in the underground tunnels, and towns like Frank, Hillcrest, Coleman and Blairmore sprang up to house the miners' families. Most of these newcomers were unsympathetic to the anti-drink crusade. They viewed a smuggler like Picariello as providing a necessary public service, not breaking a law. So indifferent were they to his extra-legal activities that the voters in Blairmore made him one of their town councillors. In the summer of 1920 the town's opera house was the scene of a "bootlegger's ball," hosted by local liquor smugglers to raise money in support of their jailed comrades.

Using his hotel as a base of operations, Emperor Pic deployed a pair of speedy McLaughlin Six Specials to haul his cases of illicit booze across the border from BC and Montana. Known as "Whisky Sixes," the roomy, powerful McLaughlins were the favourite motor vehicle for smugglers operating on the dusty backroads of Canada's western borderlands. It was said that in Picariello's case the bumpers of his vehicles were reinforced with concrete to make it easier for him to smash through police roadblocks. He excavated a tunnel under the hotel so that he could make deliveries

out of sight of police spies, and installed a player piano in the lounge to cover up the sound of clinking bottles as cases were loaded and unloaded. The Alberta Provincial Police (APP), which was created in 1917 to replace the North West Mounted Police in the province, made attempts to stop the liquor traffic but without adequate numbers or popular support, there wasn't much the force could do.

Picariello was joined in the business by his son Stefano, who regularly drove one of the big McLaughlins, often accompanied by young Florence Lassandro, wife of one of Emperor Pic's henchmen and a waitress at the hotel. On September 21, 1922, three cars arrived in Blairmore with a shipment of liquor from Fernie. Acting on a tip, two APP officers appeared at the hotel and handed the Emperor a search warrant. Before they could proceed inside, Picariello honked his horn in warning and Stefano sped away in one of the other cars. The police followed, as did the Bottle King, who managed to place his automobile between Stefano and his pursuers, keeping them at bay until finally they called off the chase. Stefano continued to race toward the BC border. As he passed

The unfortunate Florence Lassandro was only twenty-two years old when she hanged alongside Emilio Picariello in 1923. She was the only woman ever executed in Alberta. At the time it was usual to commute the death sentence for women; it had been more than two decades since the last woman had been hanged in Canada. But an exception was made in the case of Lassandro, perhaps because her victim was a police officer.

through Coleman, Constable Stephen Lawson, who'd been warned he was coming, fired at the fleeing vehicle, wounding Stefano in the hand but not stopping him. At this point Picariello drove up and Lawson warned him that he should bring in his son or the police would. Later that day Picariello learned that Stefano had been wounded and arrested and he set off to find Lawson, taking the twenty-two-year-old Florence with him. Both were armed. He drove to Coleman and outside the police barracks he and Lawson had a conversation that escalated into an argument. Picariello reached for his gun, possibly to force Lawson into the car to take him to free Stefano, and the two men struggled. Shots were fired and one of them struck Lawson, who fell dead in the street in front of two of his children who were watching from the barracks.

Lassandro and Picariello fled the scene but the next day police tracked them down. The fatal bullet apparently came from Lassandro's gun but they were both charged with murder. Picariello might have got off if he had chosen to be tried separately but the story goes that he refused. "He said it was he who got Florence Lassandro into the mess," a

friend later reported, "and he was not going to save himself by letting her be convicted..." (Another, less gallant, version of the story has Picariello convincing Lassandro to take the blame for the murder because, he said, the system would never hang a woman.) During a five-day trial in Calgary the two pleaded self-defence but the jury found them guilty and they were sentenced to death. Appeals went all the way to the Supreme Court of Canada, to no avail, and on May 2, 1923, the pair were hanged at the jail at Fort Saskatchewan, near Edmonton. Lassandro was the only woman ever executed in Alberta. As she went to the gallows she is reported to have cried out: "Why do you hang me when I didn't do anything? Is there no one here who has any pity?"

Six months after the execution Albertans went to the polls in a plebiscite to decide whether to continue their experiment with prohibition. The violence associated with its enforcement was turning more and more people against the law, and prominent voices were raised in support of "moderation" instead of suppression. Given a choice of four options, voters endorsed a system of government-controlled liquor stores and the

reopening of the bars. In May 1924, Alberta officially went from dry to wet.

■ THE PICARIELLO CLAN, WHO WERE local legends in the folklore of southern Alberta, were typical, small-time liquor smugglers during the years of prohibition in Canada. On a different scale altogether were the Bronfman brothers – Harry, Abe, Sam and Allan – from Brandon, Manitoba. Beginning modestly as hotel keepers, the Bronfmans expanded into importing, exporting into the US and eventually distilling, using experience gained in the rough-and-tumble world of western whisky smuggling to establish the largest liquor empire in Canada.

Yechiel and Minnie Bronfman, patriarch and matriarch of the clan, came to Canada from Bessarabia, a province of the Russian Empire, settling on a farm near Wapella, Saskatchewan, in 1889. The homesteading experiment was not successful and three years later the family moved to Brandon where Yechiel scratched a living from a variety of businesses, including selling firewood and frozen fish. Eventually he amassed enough money to set up the eldest sons,

BELOW The Alberta Provincial Police called on the RCMP to assist in the pursuit of fugitives Florence Lassandro and Emilio Picariello, the "well known bootlegger" mentioned in this telegram. The APP had replaced the North West Mounted Police as the provincial police force in Alberta in 1917 and remained in existence until 1932, when the RCMP resumed jurisdiction.

RIGHT This is the roadblock that police set up to stop Stefano Picariello as he fled from Blairmore back into British Columbia.

CANADIAN PACIFIC R'Y. CO.'S TELEGRAPH
TELEGRAM
FORM T. D. 1

CABLE CONNECTIONS TO ALL PARTS OF THE WORLD
J. McMILLAN, General Manager of Telegraphs, Montreal.

A70 RN J   64 COLLECT NL NL

LETHBRIDGE ALTA SEPT 22-22

Provincial Const Lawson —
Murder of

THE COMMISSIONER R C M P,
OTTAWA.

CONSTABLE LAWSON OF ALBERTA PROVINCIAL POLICE MURDERED AT COLEMAN BY

WELL KNOWN BOOTLEGGER AND WOMAN LAST NIGHT BOTH ESCAPING PROVINCIAL

POLICE INSPECTOR URGENTLY REQUESTED OUR ASSISTANCE AS A MATTER OF

EMERGENCY I SENT TWELVE MEN TO ASSIST IN HUNT FOR

MURDERERS HAVE JUST RECEIVED WORD THAT MAN CAPTURED BY TWO

OF OUR MEN AND ONE PROVINCIAL POLICEMAN WOMAN STILL AT LARGE

REPORTS FOLLOWING.   CHRISTEN JUNGET.

1043PM

These labels indicate the kinds of beer brewed in Western Canada in the early years of the twentieth century.

1 • The Fernie-Fort Steele Brewing Co. originated in Fort Steele, BC, in 1898 and moved to Fernie three years later. A reconstruction of the brewing operation may be visited at Fort Steele Heritage Town. It was one of four breweries in the Kootenay area, all of which sold beer into Alberta. Note the label's use of the maple leaf emblem, already a symbol of Canada.

2 • Golden Lion Brewing Co. was incorporated in Prince Albert, Saskatchewan, in 1905, the same year the territory became a province. It remained in operation until the end of World War I when it fell victim to prohibition.

2 •

BREWING WESTERN CANADA

1 •

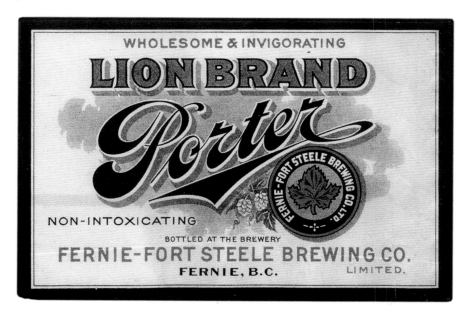

3 · The Regina Brewing Company operated from 1907 until World War I.

4 · The Saskatoon Brewing Company marketed its brew as "Liquid Bread," highlighting the supposed nutritional value of its product. Note the use of two venerable Canadian symbols, the First Nations chief and the maple leaf.

5 · Calgary Brewing and Malting Co. operated independently from 1892 until it merged with a larger consortium in 1961.

6 · The Saskatoon Brewing Company liked to feature images of a First Nations chief on its labels, suggesting that the product was "natural" and local.

7 · Another label from Prince Albert's Golden Lion Brewing.

8 · The Red Wing Brewing Co. in Prince Albert, Saskatchewan, boasted that its beer was "healthful, refreshing, nutritious."

3 ·

4 ·

5 ·

6 ·

7 ·

8 ·

ABOVE **Malt extracts, a brewing by-product, were marketed as nutritional supplements. As medicinal products, they were exempt from the prohibition laws and were sold through pharmacies. Both of these examples were made by Sleeman's brewery in Guelph, Ontario.**

OPPOSITE **The Summit Hotel in Crowsnest Pass, Alberta, lay astride the border with BC. The hotel, established in 1899, boasted a popular bar and a menagerie of animals on display, including wolves, a mountain lion and a bear. It is shown here in 1912, a few years before liquor smuggling began to rival coal mining as the preferred occupation of the area. The vehicle on the right may well have been used to run liquor from one jurisdiction to another.**

Harry and Abe, as hotel owners in nearby Emerson. (Sam got his own hotel in 1912 at the age of twenty-three.) This was the first of what eventually became a chain of Bronfman-owned hostelries in Yorkton, Saskatchewan; Winnipeg; and Port Arthur, Ontario. The real profit centres for the hotel operations were the attached barrooms, which is where the brothers were introduced to the booze business. Fuelled by the surge in immigration, the Prairie West boomed in the years leading up to the outbreak of World War I and so did the fortunes of the Bronfman family. But any boom is just a bust waiting to happen and when the bad times arrived in 1913 they hit the hotel business hard, especially after the introduction of prohibition reduced the barrooms to selling nothing stronger than a watered-down "near beer," the only drink that was still legal. Looking around for more lucrative opportunities, the Bronfman brothers hit on the liquor business. In 1916 Sam travelled east to Montreal, where retail sales were still legal, purchased a small liquor outlet and a warehouse, and launched the brothers into the interprovincial package trade, meaning that they shipped liquor from Montreal to

warehouses that they set up across Western Canada. From there it was delivered directly to customers. The operation was quite legal – in each of the Prairie provinces the importation of liquor was allowed even after the introduction of prohibition – and for a couple of years it made the Bronfmans a lot of money. When the federal government in 1918 banned the importation of alcohol as well as its consumption and sale, the brothers simply found another loophole. This time it was the exemption in all the prohibition legislation that allowed alcohol to be sold as "medicinal spirits" for ostensibly medical purposes. They established the Canada Pure Drug Company in Yorkton and began supplying alcohol to pharmacists, either straight up to be prescribed by sympathetic doctors for all manner of imaginary ailments, or as an ingredient in a wide assortment of elixirs, potions and cures that had a sometimes surprisingly high alcohol content.

Once the ban on importation lapsed at the end of 1919, the Bronfmans reactivated their mail-order business, opening a string of warehouses that ran all the way west to Vancouver. When American prohibition arrived at the beginning of 1920, these

LEFT One of the challenges faced by liquor smugglers in Western Canada was the abysmal state of the roads, especially the ungravelled backroads they were forced to use to avoid the authorities, and especially in rainy season when a vehicle, like this one, could easily get mired in the mud.

BELOW Breakdowns were another occupational hazard for the smuggler. Here a pair of liquor agents seize a truck loaded to the roof with crates of booze and masquerading as a "taxicab" when it got a flat tire.

facilities doubled as "export houses" for the distribution of booze into the US. American bootleggers arrived in their fast cars to take delivery before scooting back across the border. Again, this export trade was perfectly legal, at least on the Canadian side of the border. There were huge profits to be made and equally large risks to be run, what with law enforcement patrolling the backroads and armed hijackers waiting to relieve the smugglers of their illicit cargo. Most everyone involved in the traffic was armed to the teeth and the little warehouses – known as boozoriums – were fortified with padlocked doors and iron bars on the windows. "You could call them miniature forts," said one Saskatchewan liquor official.

The 1920s brought "car culture" to Canada and the use of automobiles to smuggle cargo south added to the romance of the enterprise. The number of motor vehicles in the country was climbing rapidly, but they were not yet an everyday sight, especially in the small towns of the hinterland. For someone who did own a car, there were hardly any roads on which to drive it, especially in the winter or the rainy season. Motoring was still an adventure and it was something special to see any automobile, let alone one of the elegant Whisky Sixes, roar through town. Smugglers were associated in the public mind with this exoticism of the open road. People talked about how the getaway artists dragged lengths of chain behind their vehicles, stirring up clouds of dust to obscure their escape, or mounted bright spotlights shining out the back to blind the liquor agents during nighttime pursuits, or hid their vehicles in haystacks until the coast was clear. To make the business a little less risky, the Bronfmans promised American border runners that if the authorities seized their cars while they were on a clandestine run north of the border, the brothers would put up the money to get the vehicles released.

In order to ensure a steady supply of product, and to maximize their profits, the Bronfmans took the inevitable next step: they began producing the booze themselves. Marketed under fanciful names like "Parker's Irish Whisky," "Prince of Wales" and "Old Highland Scotch," the Bronfman brew was a mixture of raw alcohol, water, caramel for colouring, a bit of sulphuric acid and some actual whisky, imported from Britain by the boxcar load. After a false start – the

In 1922, about when this photograph was taken, Samuel Bronfman (shown with his wife, Saidye) along with his brothers was beginning the transition from Prairie liquor smuggler to respectable Eastern businessman.

initial batch turned out a nasty blue colour – the brothers got the process right and they were launched in the business that would eventually produce their huge fortune. The Bronfmans had lots of competition – in Saskatchewan alone at least twenty export houses fed the southward flow – but they were the largest operators. As Harry boasted to a Winnipeg newspaper in 1922, "the liquor business in Saskatchewan is controlled by me."

But even as he made this claim, Harry and his brothers were finding it a challenge to navigate the rocky shoals of prohibition. While the ban on liquor in the US provided the market that produced such healthy profits, in Canada lawmakers were always threatening to put suppliers like the Bronfmans out of business. The brothers used what political influence they had to keep the inspectors off their backs but pressure grew on the provincial and federal governments to control the export traffic. In 1922 the Saskatchewan legislature called on Ottawa to use its powers to close the border warehouses. The King government was still considering what to do when a shooting took place in the little town of Bienfait that struck at the heart of the Bronfman operation.

Bienfait, Saskatchewan, with its comical name (pronounced bean-fate) and out-of-the-way location tucked down in the windswept southeast corner of the province almost atop the border with North Dakota, seems like an unlikely place to be the eye of a storm involving Jazz Age gangsters and international smuggling. But history is made in unlikely places. The Bronfmans had put their brother-in-law, Paul Matoff, in charge of their liquor warehouse in Bienfait. On the night of October 4, 1922, Matoff was at the local CPR station receiving a shipment that had just arrived by train from the East. A North Dakota bootlegger named Lee Dillage was loading his share of the booze into a Cadillac when someone stuck a 12-gauge shotgun through the station window and blasted Matoff, killing him instantly. Then the assassin entered the station, scooped up the several thousand dollars that Matoff had been counting and disappeared. Dillage and his local contact Jimmie LaCoste were suspects in the case but when eventually they stood trial they were acquitted and the murderer was never found. Combined with a string of bank robberies that many people believed were linked to American bootleggers,

the murder gave the authorities the excuse they needed. Within six weeks of Matoff's death, Ottawa announced that the export houses had to close before the end of the year.

At this point the Bronfmans might have decided the liquor business was no longer for them. Their sister's husband had been murdered in cold blood; they were forced to sell off what stock they had on hand ahead of the government-mandated closures (James Gray called it "the greatest fire sale of booze in the annals of the west"); sensational press reports were linking the family to disreputable business practices and known gangsters. The pressures were so great that Harry suffered a nervous collapse. But it was part of the Bronfman genius to turn challenges into opportunities. Instead of closing up shop, the brothers simply rode off in another direction. In 1924 Sam and Harry purchased a distillery in Kentucky, moved it to Ville LaSalle just outside Montreal and incorporated a new company, Distillers Corporation Ltd. For several years they had been importing whisky from the Edinburgh-based Distillers Company Ltd. (DCL), one of the leading producers in Britain. In 1926 the Bronfmans went into

BELOW This museum piece illustrates the operations of a simple portable still. When the large canister containing the raw ingredients was heated, vapour passed through the tubes and condensed into the bucket. The resulting product could be toxic if inexpertly made; there were many instances of people being poisoned by moonshine liquor.

RIGHT Two men display an illegal still in Irricana, Alberta, northeast of Calgary, in 1922, a year in which authorities seized more than a thousand stills across the country. A small apparatus like this one probably produced moonshine, or "swamp whisky," for personal consumption with some left over for sale to the neighbours. The term "moonshine" suggests the illegality of the trade, carried out clandestinely by the light of the moon.

partnership with DCL, with the latter providing capital and a source of malt whisky in return for a fifty-percent share of the Canadian company. The new operation was immediately successful, supplying the government-operated liquor stores that were replacing outright prohibition in Canada, and exporting into the American market, which was still legal. The brothers' sometimes-suspect past as Western liquor smugglers was behind them now. The mid-1920s, Sam told a journalist, "was when we started to make our real money." So profitable was the new business, he said, that "what came out of the border trade in Saskatchewan was insignificant by comparison." In 1928 Distillers Corp. merged with Joseph Seagram & Sons of Waterloo, Ontario, to create Distillers Corporation-Seagram's Ltd., later the Seagram Company Ltd., at one time the largest distiller in the world.

■ IN THE SPRING OF 1923 THE *CHICAGO Daily News* reported that 100,000 gallons of liquor were crossing the border into the US from Canada every day, hidden underneath clothing, disguised as medicine and milk, carried by boat, canoe, train, car and even airplane, buried in bales of hay and under sacks of coal, siphoned into false gas tanks and spare tires. There were as many schemes for sneaking liquor across the border as there were fertile brains to think them up. In Ontario the main entry point for this illicit booze was the Windsor-Detroit Funnel (see Chapter One), but a second route almost as popular was the Niagara Peninsula and that is where Rocco Perri, once dubbed "Canada's Al Capone," ruled the roost.

Like Sam Bronfman, who lobbied hard for a seat in the Canadian Senate and aspired to the social status of the upper-class British distillers he did business with, Perri too used the booze business to escape a background of hard-scrabble poverty. Born in the southern Italian province of Calabria, Perri emigrated to the New World in 1903 when he was sixteen years old. After working at an assortment of menial jobs in New York State he crossed the border into Canada in 1908 and eventually found himself in the Ward, an immigrant working-class district of Toronto. This is where he met Bessie Starkman, who was operating a boarding house with her husband. Rocco convinced Bessie to leave her husband and their two

■ Almost as soon as prohibition in its various forms was introduced by the provinces it was opposed by people who thought it was too extreme, too repressive. During the early 1920s these "wets" organized into provincial chapters of the Moderation League, which advocated for government regulation of liquor sales rather than an outright ban.

The League borrowed its tactics from the prohibition crusaders of an earlier era. Members collected signatures on petitions and encouraged provincial governments to hold plebiscites asking voters if they favoured some form of regulation, usually government-operated liquor stores.

League efforts were very successful and by 1930 most provinces had adopted the government-control model.

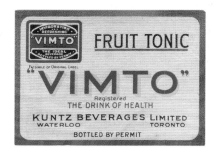

David Kuntz was a pioneer brewer in the Kitchener-Waterloo area. When his son Louis took over he renamed the operation L. Kuntz' Park Brewery. It was later owned by Carling. "Vimto" fruit tonic was one of the beverages marketed as a health drink to avoid the prohibition law.

daughters and the couple moved to St. Catharines where Rocco worked as a construction labourer on the Welland Canal. The introduction of prohibition in Ontario in 1916 found the Perris – the couple never married but lived common-law – living in Hamilton running a grocery store. Immediately they transformed the shop into an illegal drinking joint and brothel and launched themselves into bootlegging.

By all accounts, the duo were perfectly matched. Bessie was the acknowledged brains of the partnership: she kept the books, managed the money and made the deals. Retired OPP officer Charles Wood said Bessie "had a mind like a steel trap when it came to organizing the business side of their deals." Rocco took care of customer service and provided the muscle that was needed for the day-to-day operations. Short in stature – one Toronto journalist described him as "a sawed-off Mussolini" – he had an outsized personality. He smoked fat cigars, drove fast cars, drank expensive liquor and wore custom-made suits with loud silk ties. Bessie too dressed in the most stylish clothing and draped herself in jewellery. In 1920 the couple moved into a rambling

Victorian villa in a fashionable section of Hamilton with a billiard room and a hidden cellar for storing cases of booze.

The liquor traffic in southwestern Ontario was marked, in its early stages at least, by a level of violence unknown in other parts of the country. Several crime syndicates did business in the province and across the Niagara River in neighbouring upstate New York, including the Scaroni family in Guelph, the Serianni gang in Niagara Falls, New York, and Perri's outfit in Hamilton. In 1922 open warfare broke out for domination of the traffic and after a series of murders the Scaroni family was driven from the business, leaving Perri as the leading operator in the Hamilton-Guelph-Brantford area, boss of what the *Hamilton Spectator* newspaper would call "the cleverest bootlegging organization that can be found in the province." It should be emphasized that this stream of violence was fed by the most respectable connections. Perri obtained the beer and whisky that he trafficked into the US from reputable distillers Seagram's, Corby's, and Gooderham & Worts, and successful brewers like the Kuntz Brewery in Kitchener. These companies had no

The *Globe* newspaper in Toronto announces the arrival of provincial prohibition in Ontario to come into effect on September 16, 1916. The Ontario Temperance Act banned the sale of beverage alcohol and closed the bars. Ontario was the fourth province to introduce prohibition during the war – after Manitoba, Nova Scotia and Alberta – and by war's end the whole country, except Quebec, was under some form of liquor ban. No one can say whether prohibition would have been introduced without the war, but certainly the conflict seemed to give it extra urgency. As young soldiers sacrificed their lives abroad, it was felt that on the home front Canadians should be making sacrifices of their own. Giving up alcohol was considered to be one of these patriotic measures. In Ontario at least, as the newspaper story indicates, prohibition initially was intended to last until 1919. Of course, not everyone was willing to give up their daily drink and for bootleggers like Rocco Perri and Bessie Starkman, prohibition turned out to be a business windfall.

The Globe.

TORONTO, FRIDAY, APRIL 7, 1916—SIXTEEN PAGES.

VOLUME LXXIII.

NUMBER 20,962

NIGHT ATTACK BY BRITISH CARRIES TURK POSITIONS
Provincial Prohibition From Sept. 16, 1916, to June, 1919
BATTLES AROUND ST. ELOI AND VERDUN RENEWED

ANOTHER BRITISH VICTORY IN THE TIGRIS CAMPAIGN

NIGHT ASSAULT GETS FELAHIE

One Division Operates on Each Bank of River, and During Day Five Lines of Trenches Are Taken — General Gorringe, Learning That Foe Is Strongly Entrenching and Charge Must be Across Open Ground, Defers Final Attack Until Evening

ONTARIO "DRY" UNTIL JUNE, 1919

Prohibition to be Effective September 16, 1916

ANNOUNCED BY MR. HANNA

Will Give Almost Three Years of Prohibition and Fair Test — Question of Compensation for Hotelkeepers With Long Leases.

BRITISH FIGHTING AT ST. ELOI

GERMANS AGAIN FORCED BACK

French Counter-offensive Succeeds Near Douaumont

FOE STORMS HAUCOURT

HOLLAND'S QUEEN INSPECTING TROOPS

Queen Wilhelmina inspecting a frontier guard on the Belgian frontier.

P. & O. LINER SIMLA SUNK
—Presumably Used as an Allied Transport—
MANY LIVES REPORTED LOST

TRANSPORT SUNK—MANY LIVES LOST

MAJORITY OF DUTCH IN FAVOR OF ALLIES

Holland to Join U.S. in Protest Against Germany's Submarine Campaign

WAR SUMMARY

NEW FOE FORMATION SAVES FRENCH GUNS

Allied Warships Sink Foe Sub

THE NEWS OF THE DAY

LORD MONTAGU QUITS AERIAL SERVICE BOARD

SPAIN ASKS EXPLANATION

BELOW A crowd of curious onlookers watches prohibition agents and police destroy barrels of wine in 1926 in the streets of New York City. The wine, in storage since prohibition was enacted in 1920, had gone sour.

RIGHT And while liquor agents smashed the barrels, local children ran into the street with cups and buckets to scoop up as much of the illegal hooch as they could from the gutter, sour or not, to take home to their parents. The scene captures the futility of prohibition enforcement and the way it was corrupting American society.

THE HATTIE C. AFFAIR

■ MUCH OF THE LIQUOR THAT was supposedly exported to the US found its way back into Ontario with boats unloading at docks along the Lake Ontario shoreline. On the night of October 5, 1923, one of these boats, the 33-foot (10-metre) cruiser *Hattie C.* out of St. Catharines, was unloading an illicit cargo of whisky in a bay to the east of downtown Toronto. The booze, worth about a quarter of a million dollars at today's prices, had come from the Corby distillery at Belleville. Standing nearby was Rocco Perri, watching to see that his product got ashore safely.

Acting on an anonymous tip, four Toronto police officers suddenly appeared. They arrested Perri and three other men who were trying to escape into the bushes, then turned their attention to a darkened *Hattie C.*, which was backing away into the lake. When the crew aboard the cruiser ignored repeated commands to stop, all four policemen started firing their revolvers in an attempt to sink it. When the shooting stopped, the officers boarded the boat and found John Gogo dead in the arms of his father, Sydney; James Gogo, an uncle, wounded by a bullet through his

jaw; and a fourth man cowering in a corner of the cabin.

It was the first time that police had shot and killed a liquor smuggler in the province and the incident caused a sensation. The provincial attorney general appointed an inquiry to investigate the case. It revealed what everyone already knew, that Ontario distillers were ignoring the law against selling liquor for domestic consumption. At the same time, the coroner ruled that the police were not justified in shooting at the *Hattie C.* Further than that, he ruled that no officer should use a firearm to enforce the

Ontario Temperance Act. Given this opinion, the crown attorney charged the four policemen with manslaughter in the death of John Gogo. The ensuing trial resulted in a hung jury.

Meanwhile the smugglers got off with minor penalties. The charges against Rocco Perri, who claimed he was only at the scene because he was giving one of the other men directions, had to be dropped for lack of evidence.

Rocco Perri's gangland rivals finally caught up with him and Bessie in mid-August 1930 when an assassin ambushed the couple outside their Hamilton home. Rocco escaped but Bessie was fatally shot. Her funeral was considered to be the largest in the city's history, attended by thousands of curiosity-seekers attracted by the Perris' notoriety. A photographer for the *Toronto Daily Star* captured this image of Rocco collapsing in grief at the graveside.

"The law, what is the law? ... They don't want it [prohibition] in the cities. They voted against it. It is forced upon them. It is an unjust law. I have a right to violate it if I can get away with it."

– ROCCO PERRI, Hamilton gangster

compunction about selling their product to customers whom they knew full well were involved in criminal enterprises. Perri was also the supplier of choice for all sorts of respectable Hamiltonians who did not let the Ontario Temperance Act come between them and a good drink. "Many of the prominent people of the town drink," he told a newspaper reporter, "and they buy from us because they are sure that what they are getting will be good." All these activities were protected to such a degree by corrupt law enforcement and customs officials that the American consul in Hamilton, Richard Boyce, reported to his superiors that little could be done in the city to staunch the flow of illicit alcohol because the police were so heavily implicated in the traffic.

■   BY THE END OF 1924 ROCCO WAS SO confident of his immunity from the law that he gave an interview with the *Toronto Daily Star* in which he admitted to being the "King of the Bootleggers" and portrayed his business as a public service, not a crime. "The law, what is the law?" he asked the reporter. "They don't want it [prohibition] in the cities. They voted against it. It is forced

upon them. It is an unjust law. I have a right to violate it if I can get away with it... Am I a criminal because I violate a law which the people do not want?"

"I am a bootlegger," Rocco boasted. "I am not ashamed to admit it. And a bootlegger I shall remain."

Ironically, it was politics, not law enforcement, that dealt Rocco and Bessie their first setback. Even as their business affairs prospered, they became collateral damage in a scandal that came close to destroying the career of Prime Minister William Lyon Mackenzie King. King's Liberal government had barely survived the federal election of October 1925. The Liberals won fewer seats than their Conservative rivals but King, who had lost his own seat in the election, was able to cling to power by cobbling together support from the Progressive and independent members in the House of Commons. When Parliament convened in January, the wily King somehow managed to stave off repeated attempts by the Conservatives to bring down his rackety coalition. But his Achilles heel was the liquor traffic, or more accurately, the customs department that was supposed to be controlling it. It was no secret that

A man models the latest in scuba diving gear at a boathouse along the Detroit River in 1929. Presumably when he went into the river he wouldn't be wearing a heavy wool sweater! The boathouse also housed an underwater cable through which alcohol flowed between Detroit and the Ontario side, just one more ingenious technique for fooling the authorities.

many customs officials were accepting bribes from bootleggers. What's more, since smugglers liked to be able to come home with a return cargo, there was a dramatic increase in the northward traffic of contraband consumer goods out of the US, a traffic that by 1925 was estimated to total $50 million a year. In February 1926, Vancouver Conservative MP Harry Stevens stunned the House of Commons with revelations about corruption in the Montreal customs office where Joseph Bisaillon, a senior official in charge of preventing smuggling, was instead engaging in it with a vengeance: protecting bootleggers, taking kickbacks and confiscating liquor for his own use. Bisaillon even owned a farm that straddled the border between Quebec and the US and used it to smuggle goods into Canada. The trail of corruption led all the way to Ottawa and the Minister of Customs, Jacques Bureau, whom Bisaillon was supplying with liquor and, on one occasion, a smuggled automobile. None of this came as any surprise to King, who referred in his diary to the customs department as "a sink of iniquity," but he was not prepared to do much about it. Bisaillon was fired, Bureau was "retired" to the Senate and

in lieu of a full-blown Royal Commission, a parliamentary committee began hearings into the scandal.

Instead of deflating the situation, as King and his new minister of customs, George Boivin, hoped, the parliamentary committee added fuel to the fire. It concluded that the customs department was riddled with corrupt officials, once again reaching into the minister's office. During the previous election, it was revealed, Boivin had interceded to make certain that a well-known New Brunswick bootlegger and Liberal Party bagman was sprung from jail in order to work on the campaign. To make matters worse, when King tried to fire Boivin, his own MPs from Quebec would not allow it. (As it turned out, nature was able to accomplish what the Prime Minister could not; Boivin died of a ruptured appendix soon after.) King's alliance with the Progressives broke apart on the corruption issue and it seemed certain that the Liberal government would fall on a parliamentary motion of censure. With his defeat imminent, King tried to dodge the motion by asking the governor general, Viscount Byng, to dissolve Parliament so that another election could be

The scandal in the federal customs department regularly made the front pages of the nation's newspapers, as did the elusive Rocco Perri. This edition of the *Globe* from June 1927 tells of police attempts to locate Perri and his partner-in-crime, Bessie Starkman. When the Royal Commission into the scandal resulted in perjury charges against Perri, the mobster had once again gone into hiding. "All efforts to find them in their Hamilton home have failed," said the *Globe* reporter. (Eventually Perri was found and served time in prison.) Meanwhile, the main headline also refers to the Royal Commission and the evidence it revealed of tax evasion and other corrupt practices by some of the country's largest liquor companies. The photo is of Newton Rowell, a prominent Toronto lawyer and former federal cabinet minister, whom Prime Minister King had appointed chief counsel for the commission.

The Globe.

Read It in the Morning While It Is News

26 PAGES

TORONTO, SATURDAY, JUNE 4, 1927.

VOL. LXXXIV. NUMBER 24,155.

THE WEATHER
Probabilities: Partly-fair, and warmer

ROWELL DEMANDS THAT BREWERIES PAY TAX ARREARS

Arrest of Italians May Enable Police To Find Rocco Perri

BANK ROBBERY CLUE LEADS TO MONTREAL; POLICE INVESTIGATE

Criminal Prosecution Is Urged Against Certain Lawbreakers In His Scorching Arraignment

RICHES OF ROUYN AVAILABLE EARLY FOR WORLD MARKETS

SUBMITS FINDINGS

HON. NEWTON W. ROWELL, K.C.

BRITISH MINISTER LEAVES MOSCOW

ROUYN IS MENACED BY FOREST FIRES

FRENCH STEAMER HITS UNITED STATES SHIP

Old Indian on His Death-Bed Reveals Secret of Ore Find

BELOW **William Lyon Mackenzie King** campaigns from the back of an automobile in Cobourg, Ontario, during the 1926 "King-Byng" election. King was leader of the Liberal Party from 1919 to 1949 and prime minister for almost twenty-two years. He knew the customs department was rife with graft and corruption but as prime minister he had stonewalled the issue so as not to divide his government. He had also avoided shutting down the export trade that sent so much illicit liquor into the United States. Eventually King was forced to act on both fronts, setting up a Royal Commission into the customs department and, later, banning the export of alcohol to the US.

Viscount Byng, shown here with his wife in 1922, commanded the Canadian Corps during World War I, and particularly during the attack on Vimy Ridge in April 1917 for which he became known as "Byng of Vimy." He served as governor general from 1921 to 1926, leaving Canada under a cloud because of his controversial run-in with Prime Minister King. Lady Byng donated the trophy that bears her name to the National Hockey League as an annual award to the player best exhibiting sportsmanship combined with excellence.

called. When Byng refused, King resigned and Arthur Meighen took over as prime minister. Meighen's government lasted all of three days before it was defeated in the House and King got his election after all. He also got his main campaign issue, what he characterized as the high-handed abuse of parliamentary procedure by the governor general. King had obviously been trying to use Viscount Byng to dodge the censure of Parliament but during the campaign he managed to paint himself as the defender of Canadian autonomy against the perfidious misuse of power by a deluded governor general. Nothing less than Canadian independence was at stake, he blustered. This was the infamous "King-Byng Affair" and on September 26, 1926, it helped propel Mackenzie King back into power with a majority of seats.

The customs scandal was not completely forgotten during the campaign and once back in office King went ahead with the appointment of a Royal Commission to look into the corruption charges. The Royal Commission on Customs and Excise began hearings in Ottawa in November. Among the witnesses called to appear were Rocco Perri and Bessie Starkman. While Rocco's name kept popping up in testimony – surprisingly, none of the other witnesses admitted to knowing him at all! – the man himself could not be found until the following April when he emerged from hiding and both he and Bessie appeared for questioning. Predictably defiant, Rocco pooh-poohed attempts to paint him as a big-time operator. The infamous interview in the *Star* was just a spoof, he said, and he repeatedly claimed a bad memory when asked to recall specific individuals and events. Bessie, on the other hand, told bald-faced lies in court: in the most outrageous instance, when asked how much money she and Rocco had in the bank, she presented a statement for $98.78. Unhappily for the Perris, commission staff were able to find evidence that the couple had close to a million dollars in various accounts, a discrepancy that led to charges of perjury. After making a plea bargain that saw Bessie go free, Rocco was sentenced to six months in the Ontario Reformatory at Guelph, the first time that the King of the Bootleggers had seen the inside of a prison cell.

Perri's jail time would not have caused

This photograph from the *Detroit News* shows a rum-runner on a riverside dock near Windsor, Ontario, peering through binoculars to the opposite shore waiting for a signal that it is all clear to bring a boatload of booze across to Detroit.

much disruption in his business – Bessie was quite capable of carrying on without him – but prohibition in Ontario was winding down anyway. Because of testimony at the Royal Commission large companies such as Kuntz, and Gooderham & Worts, were fined hundreds of thousands of dollars for tax evasion. Legitimate manufacturers stopped supplying bootleggers with product. On June 1, 1927, the first government-run liquor stores opened in the province (though it would be another seven years before public drinking spots were legalized). And in 1930 the federal government, under pressure from the US, finally made the export of liquor to countries where prohibition was in effect illegal; in other words, the United States.

By the late 1920s the Perris had diversified into drug trafficking along with liquor smuggling and gambling. Apparently Bessie looked after the drug side of the business, which was perhaps why she was targeted. On August 13, 1930, she was gunned down as she and Rocco arrived late at night at their Hamilton residence. There were many suspects, including Rocco himself, but the identity of the murderer was never discovered, at least by the police. It is now assumed that

Bessie had reneged on a payment to her New York suppliers for a shipment of drugs. As for Rocco, he was interned for three years during World War II as an enemy alien. While he was away his place was taken by other mobsters and six months after his release, in April 1944, he disappeared. "Canada's Al Capone" was never seen again.

■ THE GREAT LAKES CONSTITUTE MOST of the international boundary between Ontario and the US. The liquor smugglers focused their activities where the lakes narrow and drain into one another – at Sault Ste. Marie, along the Detroit River and at Niagara, for instance. But for intrepid rum-runners, who knew enough of weather and navigation, and had access to a large enough boat, the daring dash across to upstate New York, Pennsylvania or Ohio was a risk worth taking.

On Lake Ontario the largest group of smugglers was organized by the Hatch brothers, Herb and Harry. When prohibition put the Hatch's Toronto liquor store out of business, Harry had gone to work for Sir Mortimer Davis, owner of the Canadian Industrial Alcohol Company (CIAC) in Montreal. CIAC operated the Corby distillery

near Belleville, and Wiser's distillery in Prescott on the St. Lawrence River about halfway between Kingston and Cornwall. When Hatch joined the company as sales manager in 1921, it became his job to find a way into the lucrative US market for illicit booze and he succeeded beyond his new employer's wildest dreams. Within two years Corby's output had increased from five hundred gallons of whisky a month to fifty thousand gallons, largely because of increased sales to American bootleggers. Harry Hatch recruited a small navy of fishermen and wharf rats to move the liquor across the lake in powerboats. At the same time, Herb had assembled his own band of rum-runners and a fleet of more than three dozen boats, which he put at the disposal of his brother.

The process was straightforward. When an order for a certain number of crates of liquor arrived at the company's head office in Montreal, along with the cash to pay for it, the order was forwarded to one of the distilleries in Ontario for fulfillment. From the distillery, crates made their way by rail to a siding at one of the lake ports where the smugglers would load them onto a boat for the trip across the lake. All the proper

◾ MAIN DUCK ISLAND IS FOUR hundred hectares of low-lying rock and forest at the eastern end of Lake Ontario not far from the international border, a convenient location for liquor smugglers needing shelter during their crossing to Oswego and other ports of entry in upper New York State. The island was owned by Claude "King" Cole who ruled Main Duck like his own principality. Cole and his family lived on the island from spring to fall raising cattle and pigs, as well as racehorses, and running a fishing operation. He owned several small cottages that he rented to fishermen, and two or three tugs that he used to haul loads of whitefish and lake trout to market.

With the introduction of prohibition in the US, Cole added smuggler to his list of occupations. He transported whisky and beer from mainland Canada to his island, then transshipped it to Oswego and up the ship canal to Syracuse, often buried under piles of fish to discourage a search. Cole ensured his success with liberal bribes paid into the pockets of US customs officials.

On one occasion the police raided Cole's home on Main Duck when the King was absent. They found thirty-two cases of bourbon along with a keg of rye, which they carted back to Belleville. At trial Cole argued that he had purchased the liquor for his own use and since he was keeping it in his home no laws had been broken. Thirty-two cases of cheap bourbon seemed like a lot of booze to keep for personal consumption; nonetheless, the judge agreed with Cole and dismissed the case. To add insult to injury, he required the police to return the confiscated liquor to Main Duck, from where the King undoubtedly moved it on to customers in New York.

Claude Cole, the "King" of Main Duck, purchased the island from the Canadian government in 1904 for $1,200 and used it as a base for his various business operations, including a lake fishery that employed this tug for moving the fish to market. When prohibition came along, he naturally began using his boats to smuggle liquor. The island was a perfect place to dodge the US Coast Guard and, when necessary, stash a shipment of booze until the heat died down.

Many of the lake's rum-runners put in at Main Duck where King Cole gave them a warm welcome. In 1941 John Foster Dulles, Secretary of State under President Dwight Eisenhower, purchased Main Duck and used it as a retreat from his public duties. Today the island, owned by Parks Canada, is back in public hands once again.

LEFT A fully loaded rum-running boat, sitting low in the water, waits beside a dock on the Detroit River waterfront.

BELOW Workers unload a boxcar full of liquor on the Detroit River waterfront. These crates would be transferred onto waiting boats that would whisk them across the river.

American customs officials examine a set of steel torpedoes found aboard one of the rum-runners. The containers were filled with alcohol and towed underwater behind the vessel, avoiding detection by prohibition patrols.

paperwork accompanied the shipment, including excise permits proving that duty had been paid and a B-13 customs form that was supposed to indicate its true destination. All of this was legal and above board, though many of the customs officials received payoffs to ensure that not too many questions were asked. It was only when the liquor-laden vessels crossed the international border in the middle of the lake that any law was broken and since that was American law no one in Canada much cared. That said, there were ways of running afoul of Canadian authorities as well. Once assembled and approved, shipments were supposed to be sealed until they reached their stated destination. It was illegal to break up a load into smaller lots for multiple customers who were not mentioned in the documents. Nor was it legal to reroute any of the booze back into Canada, though this practice, known as "short circuiting," was common.

While entrepreneurs like the Hatch brothers and the Bronfmans, or mobsters like Rocco Perri, organized the illicit liquor traffic, it was the rum-runners who actually risked their necks out on the open water. At least in the early years of prohibition, when the US Coast Guard had almost no presence on the Great Lakes, the risk of interception by law enforcement was not great. Still, the smugglers had to be prepared to jettison their cargo if they were stopped. The booze was usually carried in burlap sacks for ease of handling. Each sack contained two dozen bottles and, unlike crates, sacks sank when thrown overboard. Sometimes the cargo was carried in a net slung along the outside of the hull. If a boat was stopped, the net containing the liquor was cut away to be retrieved later. Another trick was to tie sacks onto a single line, one sack every few metres. A chunk of salt weighed down one empty sack that was tied to a marker. When the salt dissolved the bag rose to the surface, marking the spot where the rum-runner could return when the coast was clear to drag for his load. Hijackers were always a risk and most rum-runners carried shotguns and pistols with them to discourage any piracy.

For obvious reasons, rum-runners preferred to travel at night showing as little light as possible. As a result their vessels came to be called "black boats." But not every smuggler was a shrinking violet. One of the most respected operators was Bruce Lowery, a commercial fisherman from Milford, Ontario. Lowery came to rum-running reluctantly when his fishing business was foundering and a job presented itself running a whisky boat for the Belleville veterinarian and bootlegger Doc Welbanks. Lowery adopted the strategy of hiding in plain sight. He would cross to Oswego in broad daylight, using Welbanks' decrepit old fishboat, the *Rosella*, whose tiny engine cranked out so much noise and exhaust that no one suspected it of being an illegal boat on clandestine business. The ruse worked for several trips, until one day a US Coast Guard cutter seized the *Rosella* off Main Duck Island and impounded its cargo of one hundred and ten bags of beer and forty bags of liquor. Subsequently the case against Lowery was tossed out since the Coast Guard had so obviously infringed Canadian waters. Nonetheless, American customs sold the boat at auction and Welbanks found himself out of pocket several hundreds of dollars. He bided his time until later that fall the new owner of the boat, a fish buyer from Rochester, dispatched it across the lake to Deseronto, Ontario, to pick up some fish.

In the middle of the night Welbanks appeared waving a revolver and seized back his vessel, claiming it had been taken from him illegally. A Canadian court agreed, ruling that Welbanks could keep his boat, which he immediately put back to work running liquor across the lake. Bruce Lowery, meanwhile, shifted his operations to Kingston where he joined a crew running booze for Bill Fischer, a Syracuse bootlegger. By the end of the decade rum-running had become too risky for him, as it had for so many members of the rum navy. Lowery retired from the lake and ended up working for Harry Hatch in the Gooderham & Worts warehouse.

The findings of the Royal Commission on corruption in the customs department hit the Hatch operations hard. The commission revealed many of the fraudulent methods distillers were using to avoid paying taxes and duties on the liquor they sent into the US. As a result, Gooderham & Worts, the Toronto distiller that Harry Hatch had purchased in 1923, had to pay close to a half million dollars in unpaid sales tax. Worse, the Hatch brothers were both charged in the US with violating the prohibition laws, though they never stood trial. In 1926 Hatch acquired

the Hiram Walker distillery to add to his empire (see Chapter One) but before long he withdrew from regular management of the company and devoted most of his time to his stable of racehorses.

By the middle of the decade the US government decided to beef up the Coast Guard, both on the lakes and along the East Coast, in an attempt to stem the flow of booze into the country. Basically, it declared war on the smugglers. In 1925 several new vessels were deployed on the Great Lakes, armed with rapid-fire cannons, mounted machine guns and hand weapons. Some of these vessels were 75-foot (23-metre) cutters operated by a crew of eight and capable of remaining on patrol for a week at a time. Others were smaller, speedier picket boats that could chase down the smugglers in shallow coastal waters. To Canadians this "rum navy" seemed an unprecedented militarization of the Great Lakes and a violation of international law, in particular the Rush-Bagot Agreement that followed the War of 1812 and was supposed to limit the use of naval vessels on the lakes. Not so, argued the Americans; Coast Guard craft were civilian, not military vessels, a distinction

that was lost on many Canadians. By 1929 there were more than one hundred American vessels deployed on the Great Lakes in the fight to stop the liquor traffic. It was the largest naval force that the US had ever stationed on the lakes. As some of the rum-runners armed themselves to fight back, the much-vaunted "undefended border" threatened to become a war zone.

The Americans coupled this enforcement initiative with diplomatic pressures on the Canadian government to clamp down on the liquor traffic. The US wanted the right to pursue suspected rum-runners back into Canadian waters, an obvious violation of Canadian sovereignty. Prime Minister King resisted. The treasury took in a significant amount of revenue each year from taxes levied on liquor destined for the US. By the late 1920s this figure reached close to $9 million, a windfall that any government would be reluctant to give up. Nor did the prime minister want to appear to be giving in to American bullying. Canadians were not breaking the law; it was up to the Americans to police their own border and this did not include "invading" Canadian space. Several well-publicized incidents heightened

DEATH OF A RUM-RUNNER

■ BEN KERR WAS A PARTICULAR thorn in the side of the US Coast Guard. He was a fearless man – his biographer calls him "Canada's most daring rum-runner" – who made no bones about what he did for a living and promised to keep on doing it no matter what the authorities did to try to stop him.

Kerr was a plumber by trade but the postwar recession left him down on his luck with a family to support so he turned to rum-running, sometimes for his fellow Hamiltonian, Rocco Perri. In 1926 Kerr commissioned a sleek new cabin cruiser from the Morris Boat Works in Hamilton. The *Pollywog* was a 40-foot (12-metre), cedar-plank beauty with a shiny black hull sheathed in steel to protect it from the ice, mahogany trim and twin engines that could drive it across the lake at a top speed of 65 km/h. Kerr put the new boat to work running as many as ninety cases of whisky at a time to the many clandestine landing spots he knew on the south shore of Lake Ontario.

Kerr was one of the smugglers who braved the ice and the freezing cold all winter. In late February 1929, after dropping off a shipment on the New York side, he and his partner, Alf Wheat, disappeared. Friends scoured the ice-choked lake but found no trace of the missing boat. A month later the bodies of Kerr and Wheat were found washed ashore near Colborne, east of Cobourg. They were so mutilated that they had to be identified by their tattoos. The *Pollywog* may have gone down in a storm – a coroner ruled accidental death – but many people believed that the two men were murdered by hijackers.

Prohibition was lucrative for Ben Kerr. With the profits he made running illicit booze he rescued his business, built a large home in Hamilton, even bought himself a hockey team. Kerr is shown here, with the team, second from right in the fur coat.

BELOW **Canadians crossing into the US were subjected to careful scrutiny by US Customs agents. While most illegal liquor was smuggled in large quantities by boat, train or truck, individual drivers were also suspect. Here an agent questions a motorist while his partner inspects the "trunk" for contraband.**

RIGHT **The Americans' willingness to use violence against Canadian rum-runners was a cause of friction between the two governments and contributed to efforts to defuse tensions along the border. Note the bullet holes in the windows of this vessel, captured by the US Coast Guard after a chase.**

As smuggling along the coast and across the Great Lakes increased, so did the vigilance of the US Coast Guard. Here a crew member gets training in the use of the one-pounder gun used to fire on boats suspected of carrying loads of liquor across the border from Canada.

tensions between the two countries as the US Coast Guard fired on Canadian boats and made incursions into Canada in pursuit of alleged bootleggers.

In January 1930 the Americans announced that they intended to reinforce the border with a huge increase of ten thousand armed agents. In the face of this escalation, fearful that it might lead to more violence, deaths, even hostilities between the two countries, and sensitive to criticism that he was in cahoots with the liquor traffickers, Prime Minister King softened his stand and agreed, finally, to ban liquor exports from Canada. The required legislation passed into law shortly before the July election which saw King's Liberal government replaced by R.B. Bennett and his Conservatives. With the ban in force, rum-running was now illegal in Canada and the US. Not only did smugglers have to dodge the US Coast Guard, they also had to contend with the RCMP, provincial and municipal police and the Customs Preventive Service. As a result, many smugglers on the Great Lakes retired from the business.

■ IT IS PROBABLY NO ACCIDENT THAT the northwest corner of New Brunswick was home to one of the most notorious bootleggers in all of Canada. Madawaska County, the "New Brunswick Panhandle," had revealed its independent streak long before prohibition. During colonial times it had been occupied by French settlers, both Acadians and Québécois, but it was unclear what the boundaries were and who had jurisdiction over the area: Quebec, New Brunswick or the US. During the 1830s the government of Maine began to assert its claim, even promising to send soldiers to occupy the Madawaska, where loggers had begun stripping timber from the thick forests. In response the British dispatched the New Brunswick militia to oppose the Americans. Early in 1839 groups of lumbermen from Maine and New Brunswick threatened to come to blows over who had the right to cut timber in the valley of the Aroostook River, a tributary of the Saint John. British and American troops shouldered their rifles but negotiators calmed the situation and the so-called "Aroostook War" never actually broke out. In 1842 the US and Britain agreed on a boundary for the Madawaska, though the independent spirit of the county is reflected in the legendary "Republic of

These labels are from two examples of "near beers" or "temperance beers" produced in Ontario by the Kuntz Brewery of Waterloo. Both labels substitute the words "malt beverage" for beer.

In 1924 Premier Howard Ferguson increased the allowable alcohol content of beer from 2.5 percent to 4.4 percent as a step away from strict prohibition.

■ Ontario Conservative leader Howard Ferguson led his party to victory in the provincial election of 1923 partly on a platform of restrained prohibitionism. He criticized the hard line taken by former Attorney General Raney, but he was not prepared to make Ontario wet without consulting the voters once again in a plebiscite. In October 1924 Ontarians voted on the issue and upheld prohibition by a small majority.

Acknowledging that people were moving toward loosening up the law, Ferguson decided to allow the sale of stronger beer. "Near beer" with a 2.5-per-cent alcohol content had been allowed since the beginning of prohibition. Now the government would permit a beverage that was 4.4 percent alcohol. "Fergy's Foam," as wags called it, won more ridicule than support. Thirsty Ontario drinkers found it weak and watery. When a brewer offered a hundred-dollar prize to the first person who could get drunk on it, the cash went unclaimed.

After another provincial election victory, Ferguson introduced government liquor stores to Ontario on June 1, 1927.

London's Carling Breweries manufactured this "light ale" featuring an alcohol content with the approved amount of 2.5 percent. Curiously, it was marketed as a "family beverage."

Madawaska," which despite being a republic of the imagination has its own flag, its own capital (Edmunston), even its own honorary president. It is this renegade spirit of pride and independence that nourished Albenie Violette, known sometimes by his nom de commerce, "Joe Walnut."

To call Violette a bootlegger hardly does him justice. He was a captain of industry, a merchant prince, at least in the eyes of his fellow Madawaskans. He owned two hotels, a car dealership, a brickyard, a woodworking factory, a bottling plant and a winter home in Florida. In Saint-Léonard, the capital of his empire, his nephew was the police chief and Violette controlled the street lights which he switched off whenever one of his shipments of contraband had to be moved. "Tall and slim, agile as a cat, dark-featured, with thin cruel lips," one of his adversaries described him, with "a fiendish temper and few scruples." B.J. Grant, historian of prohibition in New Brunswick, called him "the biggest rum-gangster in a province that had a lot of them."

Violette had been distilling and smuggling liquor long before prohibition but the 1920s were his glory days. To the police, he

was a dangerous criminal but in Madawaska he was a folk hero. His daring escapades were the stuff of legend. People talked about the time he embarrassed liquor inspectors by substituting water for whisky in six barrels they seized from the basement of one of his hotels. When the contents of the barrels were revealed in court to be non-alcoholic, Violette sued the government and won damages of more than a thousand dollars a barrel. Or they talked about the time he smashed into a border blockade in his Whisky Six; while customs officers searched the wreck, and found nothing, a truckload of booze was able to sneak past undetected. After he was dead they talked about the giant still that police had found hidden in an underground room below his barn in Saint-Léonard.

The still was the centre of one of Violette's most profitable sidelines: the importation and processing of denatured alcohol, pure alcohol to which substances had been added to make it noxious to drink. Denatured alcohol had many legitimate uses and could be imported from the US without any trouble. It turned out that Violette was bringing in barrels of the stuff, redistilling it to remove

the dangerous, foul-tasting additives, then using it to manufacture name-brand liquor that was resold at a handsome profit on the black market. On one occasion railway and liquor officials seized a boxcar at Saint-Léonard filled with eighty barrels of alcohol which a newspaper estimated would be worth a million dollars by the time it was repurposed as drinkable booze. Violette did all he could to intimidate the customs men into surrendering his shipment but for once he failed and the train car with its illegal cargo remained in the hands of the government. A newspaper reporter called it "the biggest liquor deal ever revealed in this province."

Joe Walnut may have been one of the most ambitious bootleggers in New Brunswick but he had lots of competition from smaller operators. The 513-kilometre border with Maine was designed as if for smuggling. As the Americans began their experiment with prohibition at the beginning of 1920, the *Fredericton Daily Mail* reported that "Canadian liquor in quantities from one gallon to a truckload is being hidden in the northern woods and distributed by automobile, sled and iceboat, on snow-shoes and on skis. The Canadian brand of whiskey

Albenie Violette owned several businesses in Saint-Léonard, New Brunswick, including two hotels, a garage and a Ford dealership. He imported Cuban cigars, among other things, and owned a yacht, along with several other vessels which he used to smuggle in merchandise from the islands of Saint-Pierre and Miquelon or from Jamaica. "Joe Walnut," as he was known, operated his own distillery and had a provincial permit to sell alcohol. He has been called the most successful bootlegger in New Brunswick during the prohibition era. He died in 1929.

is sold at from $15 to $20 a quart." There were a few official crossings but much of the borderland was a labyrinth of logging roads and woodland trails. One newspaper reporter estimated early in 1921 that there were about one hundred cars a day moving liquor between New Brunswick and Maine with only a handful of border agents to interfere. Often several vehicles travelled together with spotter cars sent on ahead to draw the attention of the police. If the coast was clear the message was passed back down the road and the rest of the caravan came ahead.

It was estimated that only about five percent of the booze was stopped at the border, making New Brunswick probably the most open boundary anywhere across the country. Emblematic of the porous border was the peculiar New Brunswick institution known as the line-house. This was a home or a store built right on top of the boundary line so that smuggling was as simple as crossing from one room to another. If agents on one side of the border tried to make an arrest, the miscreant simply had to jump across the room into the neighbouring country. In 1928 frustrated authorities began destroying any of the line-houses where illegal liquor was discovered and they soon disappeared from the scene.

Enforcement of prohibition in New Brunswick was initially the responsibility of government liquor inspectors who held their jobs thanks to the patronage of local politicians. Competence and honesty were not always the first qualifications to be considered, and when a government changed, so did the inspectors. The same went for the other side of the line, where enforcement officials were often in the pay of the smugglers. In Houlton, Maine, for instance, just across the border from Woodstock, it was revealed in 1923 that prominent attorney Charles Calvin was the centre of a large liquor ring being supplied by the Fredericton rum-runner Guy Anderson. Calvin got away with it because he was paying the local sheriff $625 a month to protect his runners from interference. In 1927 New Brunswick created a provincial police force, primarily to deal with the liquor traffic. The NBPP replaced the liquor inspectors but the illegal traffic went on much as before. (The RCMP took over from the provincial police on April 1, 1932.)

And it wasn't just smuggling to the US. Liquor was widely available within the

New Brunswick banned the production and sale of alcoholic beverages in 1917 and provincial prohibition remained in force for the next decade. As everywhere else in the country, determined drinkers found a way around the law. One of the most popular sources of booze was the drugstore, where pharmacists did a roaring business selling liquor disguised as medicine, all quite legally. This letter from Harry Wade, a druggist in Perth-Andover in the Saint John River Valley, is an order for twenty gallons of alcohol concealed as general freight. Wade asks his supplier to use a false name on the invoice and to make sure that all the tins are "full to the top" so that they do not "shake or gurgle" and give the game away. It has been estimated that during prohibition druggists sold as much liquor legally as the bootleggers did illegally.

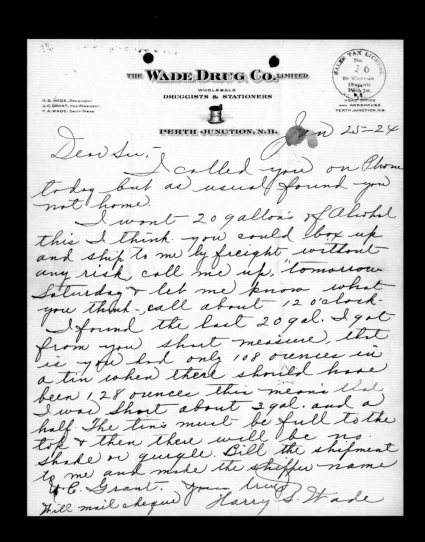

Corporals R.S. Pyne (Left) and M.F.A. Lindsay seize a homemade still at Carlyle, Saskatchewan. The RCMP were responsible for policing this side of the illegal liquor trade but they didn't get much cooperation from members of the public who saw little harm in brewing up a batch of bootleg hooch for friends and family.

province as well. According to an article in the *Moncton Daily Times,* one pharmacy located near the Saint John railway station distributed its business card to passengers on board the trains so they would know where to obtain their booze when they got to town. "Even grocery stores sold smuggled liquor," the article went on, "one Waterloo Street grocer keeping a select stock in a large office safe. Hotels, barber shops and a horde of bootleggers sold whiskey day and night and the percentage of convictions was infinitesimal." All kinds of legitimate stores and businesses doubled as fronts for bootleg operations. And the same was true of neighbouring Nova Scotia where in 1925 the inspector-in-chief reported: "So much liquor is now smuggled and distributed throughout the Province in motor cars and by bootleggers that the closing of bars and blind pigs does not have much effect on the total consumption. It is beyond the power of local inspectors to control smuggling or even to check it to any appreciable extent."

■ AS THE INEFFECTIVENESS OF PROHIBI-tion enforcement became increasingly difficult to deny, governments at last began to take measures to turn off the open spigot that was pouring booze across the border into the US. Export warehouses were closed. As distillers were taken to court for nonpayment of taxes and duties they began to cut their ties to the criminal underground. Domestically, government regulation of liquor sales took the place of outright prohibition. Police forces and the Coast Guard beefed up their efforts and began to do serious battle with the rum-runners. Finally, in 1930, the legal export of alcohol to the US was banned. All of these measures staunched the flow of illicit booze southward, though they certainly did not stop it.

Meanwhile, one of the unintended consequences of tighter enforcement across the land border was to redirect the activities of the smugglers to the "rum rows" off the Atlantic and Pacific coasts. From the outset boats had been delivering booze into the US from the shores of British Columbia, the Atlantic provinces and the French islands of Saint-Pierre and Miquelon. However, with the increased vigilance of the Rum Navy in the Great Lakes, the final act of the prohibition saga began to be played out in the rough waters along the continental coastlines.

Cornelius Krieghoff (1815–72) was a painter of everyday life in Quebec in the mid-nineteenth century. Born in Holland and educated in Germany, he came to Quebec in 1840 and made his living there painting genre scenes for tourists and wealthy patrons. Arthur Lismer, a member of the Group of Seven painters, once wrote: "Through Cornelius Krieghoff, the habitant comes to life, the landscape takes on colour, the winter is a form of national expression freed of its terrors, and painting becomes one with the cultural aspirations of the whole world... Perhaps there were better artists. But they owe a great deal to Krieghoff." The painter was a convivial habitué of the local taverns and often included his drinking companions in his paintings. "A Habitant Drinking" is presumably one of these. Today Krieghoff's canvases are worth hundreds of thousands of dollars. The obvious pleasure with which this habitant is savouring his drink suggests why temperance and prohibition were never as popular in Quebec as they were in the rest of the country.

Everybody does a little law-breaking when it suits their convenience, like jay-walking or driving over the speed limit. Anyway, breaking the law isn't really damaging. It's getting caught that causes all the trouble.

– FRASER MILES, radio operator and rum-runner

THE RUM-RUNNERS

■ IN THE SPRING OF 1923 A REPORTER from Los Angeles arrived in Vancouver to investigate the cross-border traffic in liquor and was astonished by what he found. "Here in Vancouver," he wrote, "liquor and the liquor traffic is trenchant..., it is blatant, it laughs at the American law." Venturing down into Coal Harbour he found what he called the "whiskito fleet" moored there: "halibut boats that have forsaken an honest calling – pleasure craft now used exclusively as law violators – fast, trim boats that can sail circles about the ancient obsolete American patrol boats. In the big office buildings – in dingy warehouses down-town, and along the water front you find the other element of liquor and the liquor interests – the keepers of the export houses, the firms whose only reason for existence is the fact that America is dry." The journalist ventured into a bar on Granville Street where he had no trouble at all making arrangements to buy a boatload of booze and where he was invited to inspect a warehouse filled with bottles of whisky, wine and champagne, "90 per cent of which

will ultimately be delivered unlawfully into the United States."

If the reporter was surprising his readers in Los Angeles, he was not telling Vancouverites anything they didn't already know. By 1923 the rum-running traffic out of the harbour was well established and an open secret. Reverend A.E. Cooke of the B.C. Prohibition Association had branded Vancouver, with some hyperbole, "the city of refuge for all the whisky-soaks and booze artists of the whole hemisphere." American prohibition had handed mariners in BC an incredible business opportunity. Whisky that sold for three dollars a gallon in Vancouver was selling for four times that amount in the US. Young men who could not find regular jobs in the postwar economic slump had no trouble finding work in the rum fleet. What began as a few small-time operators – the whiskito fleet – unloading crates of liquor at secluded harbours in Puget Sound, the San Juan Islands and down the coast of Washington State soon flourished as an elaborate network of ocean-going supply

Daily World

COALITION GOVERNMENT SUSTAINED

Pacifists Are Snowed Under

LABORITE IS SECOND STRONGEST PARTY

WILSON FINDS INTEREST IN LEAGUE GROWS

Findlay Arraigned In Police Court
Held for Hearing

WINS GREAT VICTORY AT POLLS

Who Is McGuinness?

Walter Findlay, BC's first Prohibition Commissioner, turned out to be a bit of an embarrassment to the provincial government. As the *Daily World* for December 28, 1918 reported, Findlay was arrested on suspicion of bootlegging himself.

The *World* was especially diligent in reporting the case because its owner, John Nelson, was a fervent prohibitionist and former ally of the disgraced commissioner.

FOX IN THE HENHOUSE

■ When British Columbia introduced provincial prohibition in 1917 the government appointed Walter C. Findlay to the position of Prohibition Commissioner, the top official in charge of enforcing the new law. The appointment seemed like a sensible one – Findlay was a leading activist in the People's Prohibition Association which had led the fight for the liquor ban – so readers of the popular press were shocked in December 1918 to read that Commissioner Findlay had been charged with bootlegging himself. Findlay was accused of illegally importing a trainload of seven hundred cases of rye from the Gooderham & Worts distillery in Toronto. The cargo was worth an estimated eighty-four thousand dollars (more than a million dollars in today's money). Obviously the prohibition movement was deeply embarrassed, but Findlay himself was unrepentant. After paying a fine of one thousand dollars he left for Seattle and refused to say who had been involved with him in the smuggling scheme. When he was called back to the province to testify at a special inquiry he kept mum. Even when subsequently convicted of breach of trust and abuse of his position, he served out his two-year prison term without ever naming names.

vessels, speedy coastal launches and a short-wave radio network that rivalled anything the Coast Guard could deploy in response.

■ RUM-RUNNING ON THE PACIFIC COAST was never as extensive or as lucrative as what took place on the East Coast, chiefly because the population was so much smaller. The largest American city on the West Coast in 1920 was Los Angeles, with a population of 576,673, followed by San Francisco (506,676) and Seattle (315,312). These were significant metropolitan areas with many thirsty customers but the demand for liquor paled compared to Eastern cities like New York, with its population of 5.6 million in 1920, or Chicago (2.7 million), or Philadelphia (1.8 million) or Detroit (almost a million). As well, the Pacific Coast is less ragged, offering fewer inlets and harbours where smugglers could go about their business, meaning that in theory at least the Coast Guard found it easier to suppress the illegal traffic. That said, the Puget Sound and San Juan Islands of northwestern Washington State were as complicated a stretch of coastline as anything the East Coast had to offer and it was there that independent operators

concentrated their efforts in the early years of prohibition.

Johnny Schnarr was typical of these intrepid freelancers. A veteran of the logging camps and of World War I, Schnarr happily traded in his faller's axe for a job aboard a small runabout operating between Victoria and northern Washington State in 1920. "Although I was never one to drink much," he explained in his memoirs, "I resented the fact that the government was the one telling me not to take a drink ... I couldn't see anything wrong with hauling liquor." Schnarr's first boat was just 18 feet (5.5 metres) long with a five-horsepower engine capable of making five knots with a following breeze. It wasn't about to outrun any patrol boat, but in those early days there were almost no patrol boats to outrun; the border was wide open. Schnarr and a helper would load seventy-five cases of liquor from a warehouse on the Victoria waterfront and be ready to set off at mid-morning to cruise across Haro Strait and through the San Juans, planning to arrive after dark at a remote beach near Anacortes, Washington. If all went well, and it usually did, they would make their drop and be back in Canadian waters by sun-up.

S- G 42724

LIQUOR CONTROL ACT OF ONTARIO
APPLICATION FOR SPECIAL SINGLE PURCHASE PERMIT

I, the undersigned _H. M. Hastings_

(Name in full)

of _Chateau Laurier, Ottawa_

(Address in full)

being the full age of twenty-one years and being resident in Ontario, hereby make application for a permit to make ONE purchase of spirituous liquor in accordance with the provisions of the LIQUOR CONTROL ACT OF ONTARIO and the Regulations made thereunder. I am not disqualified under the provisions of the said Act.

H. M. Hastings

(Signature of Applicant)

SPECIAL SINGLE PURCHASE PERMIT

THIS IS TO CERTIFY THAT the above named applicant whose signature is hereto attached, is entitled to make ONE purchase of spirituous liquor in accordance with the provisions of the LIQUOR CONTROL ACT OF ONTARIO and the Regulations made thereunder, and to have the same in his residence or as otherwise permitted by the said Act and Regulations. This permit cannot be used by any person other than the Applicant.

Issued at Store No. _5_ in _Prescott_, Ontario, this _13_ day of

Aug 193_5_ . _R. J. Alexander_

25 cents _____

(Signature of Issuer)

E. G. Oerrie

Chief Commissioner

No. of Bottles	Initials
6	G.

WARNING

LIQUOR MUST NOT BE DRUNK DURING CARRIAGE. Take purchases unopened direct to your home or room in your hotel. Drinking in motors is strictly prohibited. Punishment — Fine or Imprisonment. Drunkenness is a serious offence. This permit is personal to the permittee and is not transferable.

In Ontario, prohibition lasted from 1916, when Queen's Park introduced the Ontario Temperance Act, until 1927 when Howard Ferguson's Conservative government created the Liquor Control Board of Ontario (LCBO) and opened a chain of retail stores to sell liquor, wine and beer. The LCBO was a half-measure that ended full prohibition but stopped short of full deregulation. The emphasis was on "control." So, for instance, customers at the stores had to fill out purchase permits like this one, issued in Ottawa, in order to obtain a bottle or a case of beer. The permit admonishes consumers to "take purchases unopened direct to your home or room in your hotel."

One of the ways consumers got around prohibition, in the US and Canada, was the medical loophole. Doctors and pharmacists were allowed to prescribe alcohol to treat a variety of ailments, both real and imaginary. There is no question that the medical community believed in the tonic effect of alcohol, prescribing it in moderation for indigestion, heart disease, anemia, high blood pressure and other conditions. Even children received doses for common childhood illnesses. But there is also no question that during prohibition alcohol was heavily over-prescribed as a way of getting around the law. Doctors and pharmacists obtained special permits, like these ones from the US, that allowed them to sell liquor to their patients.

Much of the booze that was smuggled into the US was sold this way and it was the same in Canada where in Ontario alone in 1924 doctors wrote more than 800,000 prescriptions for bottles of alcohol.

The Thompson sub-machine gun was invented in 1919 by General John T. Thompson, an American army officer, and quickly caught on with prohibition-era mobsters and law enforcement who appreciated the gun's rapid automatic fire and convenient size. Originally called "The Annihilator," it became notorious as the Tommy gun, "the gun that made the twenties roar."

Schnarr recognized right away that he could do even better if he owned his own boat. He took his plans to a Japanese builder in Victoria and the result was the *Moonbeam*, 35 feet (10.6 metres) long with an eighty-horsepower car engine, able to speed along at eighteen knots, faster than any vessel the US Coast Guard had so far put into service. And when the Guard started building speedier cutters to prowl Puget Sound, Schnarr simply installed a more powerful engine in the *Moonbeam* so that he could still outrun the government boats, and the hijackers.

Schnarr and the other rum boats always worked at night and the rougher the weather the better. "On a winter's night any other small boat that was cruising those waters was almost certainly doing one of three things," he explained: "it was hauling liquor, it was looking to hijack someone else who was hauling liquor, or it was a Coast Guard cutter. In each case steering well clear was the only sensible thing to do. Any other course of action was liable to get you shot!" These tactics served him well. Until the end of prohibition forced his retirement in 1933, Schnarr made more than four hundred trips on the *Moonbeam* and subsequent, bigger

boats that he owned, not once getting caught or losing a shipment. "I was so successful," he boasted, "that the United States Coast Guard offered a $25,000 reward for the capture of my boat! But no one ever collected it."

Most of the violence associated with rum-running did not involve encounters with law enforcement. The greater danger was fellow lawbreakers, hijackers who preyed on the rum boats as they ran the liquor into shore. A small motor launch sneaking between islands under cover of darkness was a sitting duck for any gang of rip-off artists lying in wait. The most notorious case on the BC coast was the story of the *Beryl G*, a 45-foot (13.7-metre) fishboat owned by Bill Gillis who used it to make the occasional liquor run from southern Vancouver Island. In September 1924 a lighthouse keeper on Stuart Island, one of the San Juan group just across the international boundary from Sidney, found the boat abandoned on the shoreline, its cabin pockmarked with what appeared to be bullet holes and its decks smeared with blood. With the help of the American bootlegger who had dealt with Gillis, the BC Provincial Police learned that the *Beryl G* had been boarded at Sidney

Island by a trio of hard cases from the Seattle waterfront disguised as customs agents. Gillis and his seventeen-year-old son were murdered, their bullet-riddled bodies weighted and tossed overboard. The hijackers took the booze and set the boat adrift. Police eventually tracked down the murderers and arrested them; two of the three were hanged at Oakalla Prison, the other was jailed for life.

In the Pacific Northwest, Seattle was the destination for much of the liquor that Johnny Schnarr, Bill Gillis and the other smugglers snuck across the border. Unlike New York, Detroit or Chicago, Seattle did not have mobsters like Al Capone or ruthless gangs like the Purple Gang battling for control of the business. But it did have Roy Olmstead, police officer turned bootlegger. Olmstead had migrated to Seattle from his native Nebraska and in 1907, at the age of twenty-one, he joined the Seattle Police Department. Quick-witted, likeable, hard-working, the baby-faced Olmstead rose quickly through the ranks to become the youngest lieutenant the force had ever seen. So it came as some surprise to his fellow officers in March 1920 when Lieutenant Olmstead was found with a gang of men

Obviously not all the liquor consumed in the US during prohibition was imported from Canada. Much of it was homemade, in liquor stills similar to this one, confiscated by the authorities in Seattle, c. 1921.

off-loading a cargo of illicit liquor from a boat in a secluded cove north of Seattle. The chief of police kicked Olmstead off the force and the disgraced lieutenant had to pay a fine of several hundred dollars but there was no jail time; instead Olmstead was freed up to engage in rum-running full time. He began building a supply network reaching north into Canada, a network of so many drivers, boatmen, mechanics, scouts and warehousemen that he became one of the city's main employers. Olmstead was a frequent visitor to Vancouver where he came to arrange his booze shipments, checking into the Hotel Vancouver under the name "Mr. Potter." (In fact, Olmstead met his second wife, Elsie Campbell, on one of his business trips to the city.) In Seattle he used his profits to put policemen, sheriff's deputies, prohibition agents, even the police chief and the mayor, on his payroll. (It didn't hurt that his two brothers were senior members of the force.) Olmstead had so many officials looking the other way that at times he was able to unload shipments of booze in broad daylight on the downtown waterfront. Olmstead's operation supplied the best hotels and restaurants. He prided

himself on only dealing in quality liquor, he never allowed his men to carry guns, and he never got mixed up in drugs or prostitution, all of which earned him a reputation as "the good bootlegger." (Though Johnny Schnarr had a different opinion. In his memoirs, Schnarr portrays Olmstead as a shyster who could not be trusted to pay for his deliveries. After being cheated out of his payment twice, Schnarr swore never to haul for the Seattle bootlegger again.)

Olmstead's career on the other side of the law was brought to a close by a remarkable new surveillance technology: wiretapping. Late in 1924 federal agents raided several of Olmstead's distribution sites and arrested the man himself. They had placed wiretaps on his phones and the phones of several of his confederates and gathered volumes of incriminating evidence. His wife, Elsie, was also arrested, on suspicion of making broadcasts from a radio station Olmstead owned, directing the rum-runners where to make their landings. Released on bail to await trial, Olmstead went right back to bootlegging, this time working out a plan to bring liquor south from Canada by rail. He was caught again. In the end he was

BELOW Roy Olmstead disembarks from the ferry bringing him to Seattle from the McNeil Island Penitentiary following his release in 1931. By this time a convert to Christian Science, he spent the rest of his life operating a ministry and counselling prison inmates and ex-convicts.

RIGHT Elsie Campbell, Roy Olmstead's second wife whom he met in Vancouver, broadcast children's stories over the family-owned radio station located in their home. During World War I, Elsie had worked for British intelligence and she put her experience to good use assisting her husband. Police believed her broadcasts were coded messages beamed at the rum-running fleet and arrested her along with Olmstead, but a jury acquitted her.

VANCOUVER BREWERIES LIMITED

TELEPHONES
BAY. 4200
4201
4202

CABLE ADDRESS. BREWERIES
CODES
BENTLEYS PREFERRED
A.B.C. FIFTH EDITION
IMPERIAL COMBINATION

CANADA CREAM STOUT — CASCADE BOTTLED BEER — U.B.C. BOTTLED BEER — PILSENER BOTTLED BEER — OLD COUNTRY ALE

2700 YEW STREET

Vancouver, B.C.

THE VANCOUVER BREWERIES

LIMITED

RED CROSS BREWERY.

TRADE MARK

DOERING & MARSTRANDS BREWERY.

TELEPHONE
429.

POST OFFICE
MOUNT PLEASANT.

Vancouver, B.C. _____ 190 __

convicted of liquor charges on the basis of the wiretaps that were controversially allowed to be placed in evidence. (Mrs. Olmstead got off.) His appeals went all the way to the Supreme Court, arguing that wiretaps were an unconstitutional infringement of privacy, but they failed and Olmstead eventually served four years in prison. He later received a presidential pardon and a refund of his $8,000 fine. During his time in custody he converted to Christian Science and after his release he spent the rest of his life advocating for the church and counselling prison inmates.

■ AS TIME PASSED, CONTROL OF THE illegal traffic in BC shifted to a small number of export cartels based in Vancouver and managed by prominent members of the local business community. One of these was Consolidated Exporters. Consolidated operated out of a central warehouse on Hamilton Street, though it had a warehouse in Victoria as well, and got much of its product from United Distillers, a large distillery located near the south end of Granville Street in Marpole overlooking the Fraser River. Another was Pacific Forwarding, the

export arm of the Reifel family's two distilleries and four breweries. These operators developed an elaborate system for moving hundreds of thousands of cases of liquor into the US at one time. Large "mother ships" positioned themselves off the coast of California and Mexico just outside the territorial limit, their holds crammed with cases of whisky, rum, gin and wine, and barrels of beer. Under cover of fog or darkness, smaller, speedier boats, sometimes called "mosquito boats," made their way out to the mother ships, took on their orders, then hurried back to a secluded cove on shore to transfer the contraband to waiting trucks. The large vessels remained at sea for months at a time and were re-supplied by intermediate vessels, launches from 60 to 80 feet (18 to 25 metres) long, which brought food, fuel, mail for the crew, and more crates of liquor down from British Columbia.

Initially the territorial limit was 3 miles (4.8 kilometres) but in 1924 the US Coast Guard began to enforce a 12-mile limit (19.3-kilometre) – "or the distance that can be traversed in one hour by the vessel concerned" – in the hopes of making it more difficult for the smaller rum boats to make

Consolidated Exporters, one of the large export cartels shipping alcohol to the US, worked out of this warehouse on Hamilton Street in downtown Vancouver, though it also had offices in South America, the Caribbean, even China. By the late 1920s, Consolidated controlled most of the fleet of ships running liquor south of the border.

LEFT **On this trip in 1932 the decks of the** *Malahat* **are crowded with 55,000 cases of contraband liquor. The cases were kept on the main deck for easy access when the speedy shore boats came along- side to take on cargo.**

QUEEN OF THE RUM FLEET

■ The most infamous of the "mother ships" was the *Malahat*, a five-masted schooner built in Victoria in 1917 as a lumber carrier. The *Malahat* was 246 feet (75 metres) long, with a hull made of stout planks of Douglas fir, and when fully loaded it held 60,000 cases of liquor. It has been calculated that the *Malahat* delivered more illegal booze than any other vessel involved in the trade but in Fraser Miles's opinion its reputation as the "queen" of the fleet was a bit over-blown. "She was a shabby old ship – the owners were as tight with paint as they were with sailors' pay," Miles wrote in his memoirs. Following its adventures in the rum trade, the *Malahat* went on to have a second career carrying lumber for the Gibson family who ran logging operations on the west coast of Vancouver Island. The Gibsons used it as a self-propelled log barge, the first on the coast. Once the engines were removed it continued to be used as a barge until 1944 when it foundered in Barkley Sound. The hulk was removed to the mill town of Powell River where it joined several other wrecks to form a breakwater.

the trip from shore. Coast Guard cutters were known to ignore even this more elastic limit when it suited their convenience. Early in 1925 the Guard boarded a mother ship, the *Coal Harbour*, off San Francisco and took it under tow, claiming that Captain Charles Hudson had allowed his vessel to stray into American waters. The case was dismissed when witnesses were able to prove that the ship was well outside the limit when it was seized.

Hudson became a leading figure in Vancouver's rum-running trade. He was a decorated veteran of the Royal Navy who had come to Canada from Britain following World War I. After he failed to make a success of farming in Manitoba he moved west to Vancouver where he used his naval experience to get into rum-running. Follow-ing his stint on the *Coal Harbour* he became general manager of Consolidated Exporters. Described by one writer as "the true Master Mind of Rum Row," Hudson organized the complicated logistics of handling orders, dispatching boats, hiring crews and keeping his "fleet" supplied, all the time dodging a vigilant Coast Guard. "We operated perfectly legally," Hudson insisted to an interviewer.

"We considered ourselves public philanthro-pists." Plus, he added, the rum-runners brought prosperity back to the Port of Vancouver. "We spent a fabulous amount of money," Hudson boasted, "building boats, purchasing and overhauling engines, buying food and supplies for our ships, using the ship-yards for overhaul and in wages for the crews and for fuel." He may have been inflating the economic importance of rum-running but Hudson had a point. The liquor traffic gave a significant boost to a local economy that was in the doldrums in the early 1920s. Unemployed veterans still flooded the job market, along with the munitions and shipyard workers who had been laid off as their industries contracted. During the winter of 1921–22 hundreds of jobless men were installed at a military-style relief camp at Hastings Park where they were paid twenty cents an hour to perform menial work. Crewing for a rum-runner would have seemed like a plum job to these unfortunate victims of the postwar recession.

The pay was excellent. Fraser Miles, who joined the crew of a supply vessel in 1931, reported being paid $375 for "three months' easy work," good money when the

Rum-runners sometimes went to extremes to avoid capture by the US Coast Guard. In 1923 the crew of the *Linwood* set fire to their vessel so as to destroy the incriminating evidence.

average annual wage for a factory worker in Canada was between $850 and $1,000, not to mention that the Depression had started and work of any kind was hard to come by. On his final trip, which lasted ten months, Miles received $1,500, enough to pay his tuition so he could go to college. Clarence Greenan, a deckhand on one of the mother ships, reported being paid over $200 a month and $450 for each trip he made driving one of the speedboats to shore with a load. Johnny Schnarr recalled that he was making more than $1,000 a month as part of a two-man crew making regular trips to the San Juans. It is not difficult to see why men jumped at the chance to be involved in the business. As Captain Hudson explained: "In the Navy during the war one was shot at for years, for small pay, and if lucky one got a decoration. Rum running seemed to pay good wages for little danger and not much work, and it was fun!"

Not always fun, perhaps. Fraser Miles discovered that the work could be deadly monotonous some of the time and deadly dangerous at others. On his first trip out into the Pacific on the *Ruth B*, a 61-foot (18.5-metre) fish packer powered by a one-hundred-horsepower diesel engine, a fierce gale hammered the boat for three days. "The ocean was a heaving waste of foam and flying spray," Miles wrote. "I timed the waves. At the worst, near the end, seven huge rollers passed under us a minute, over four hundred an hour, more than ten thousand a day, endlessly riding up the front of a white wall of water, and diving down the back. The novelty of this wears off pretty fast." Still, like Captain Hudson, Miles had no trouble justifying his career outside the law. "Everybody does a little law-breaking when it suits their convenience, like jay-walking or driving over the speed limit. Anyway, breaking the law isn't really damaging. It's getting caught that causes all the trouble."

Surprisingly, rum vessels weren't caught very often. The seizure of the *Coal Harbour* was more the exception than the rule. Another notorious capture occurred in 1924 near the Farallon Islands off San Francisco. The *Quadra* was a former lighthouse tender and ore carrier once captained by John Walbran, author of the classic reference book *British Columbia Coast Names, 1592–1906*. The 175-foot (53.3-metre) steamer had fallen on hard times when it was chartered by liquor interests in Vancouver to carry a load of twenty-two thousand cases of wine, liquor and beer to Mexico. Or at least that is where the manifest said the vessel was going. Before *Quadra* had even left the Strait of Juan de Fuca it was off-loading cases onto mosquito boats that came out from the Olympic Peninsula and Puget Sound to rendezvous with it. Level with Portland there was another flurry of visitors and then the vessel made its way to the Farallons where it rode out a bad storm for a week. After resupplying from the *Malahat*, the *Quadra* had the misfortune to encounter the Coast Guard cutter *Shawnee*, which was out looking for it. A shore boat that was taking on booze tried to escape but the Coast Guard vessel brought it to a stop with a shot across its bow. After taking on board the crew of the smaller craft, the *Shawnee* turned its attention to the *Quadra*. Coast Guard Commander Howell ordered Captain George Ford to take the vessel into port, an order that Ford refused to obey, claiming he was outside American waters. Ignoring the niceties of the law, Howell sent an armed boarding party onto the *Quadra* and towed it and the shore boat to San Francisco.

ABOVE AND LEFT **Aboard the US Coast Guard cutter USS Seneca, prohibition agents examine barrels and crates of alcohol confiscated from a rum-runner in the mid-1920s. It was the** *Seneca* **that captured the notorious Captain Bill McCoy, reputed to be the inventor of Rum Row and one of the pioneers of the rum-running trade. In November 1923 the** *Seneca* **seized McCoy's vessel, the** *Tomoka*, **with two hundred cases of whisky on board.**

BREWERS, BOOTLEGGERS AND BALLROOMS

■ The Reifel family belonged to one of the syndicates that dominated the Vancouver liquor trade. Henry Reifel had come to North America from his native Germany in 1886. Two years later he and his brother Jack arrived in Vancouver and began a small brewery on Main Street that eventually evolved into Vancouver Breweries. Henry's two sons, George and Harry, both trained to be brewers and entered the family business. The Reifels took good advantage of prohibition to make a fortune not just in beer but in distilling as well. Some of this fortune had to be repaid to the American government in 1934 when the Reifels, charged in the US with smuggling, agreed to pay the American government a half million dollars in back taxes and fines.

George used the income earned from rum-running to finance an opulent lifestyle, including a Spanish colonial mansion, Casa Mia, overlooking the Fraser River, with eight bedrooms, eight bathrooms and a ballroom in the basement. (Brother Harry had his own mansion down the street.) George also invested in Vancouver's nightlife by building the Commodore Ballroom, a legendary nightspot known for its sprung dance floor and big-name musical acts.

It was said that the half million dollars worth of liquor that was found on board was the largest haul by the Coast Guard to that time. The liquor barons in Vancouver ensured their captured crew had a good time while they were in custody. "We lived like lords in San Francisco," reported one of the mates. "We had the best of food, lived in hotels, and had to report to the authorities during the day." The crew eventually got back to BC but not so the *Quadra*. As the court case dragged on, the old steamer sank at its moorings and was sold for scrap.

One of the technological innovations that Hudson and the other rum-runners used to avoid being captured like the *Quadra* was shortwave radio. Radio operators were crucial to the success of clandestine smuggling trips. Fraser Miles had never been to sea before but when a local smuggler discovered he knew how to operate a shortwave set young Miles was hired on the spot. When his boat left Vancouver, Miles didn't even know where he was going or what the purpose of the voyage was; all he knew was that he had to keep the radio working. The rum-running fleet was connected by a shortwave network. Transmissions from

"head office" in Vancouver contained coded directions about where to make deliveries and when. Most of these messages came from a radio setup hidden in an upstairs room in a private home on the west side of Vancouver. Even when the Coast Guard was able to intercept the broadcasts, decode them and pinpoint the location of the vessels, it didn't really matter. "With so many rum runners at sea," explained Miles, "especially the fast Canadian shore boats, knowing where any given rum-running ship was did not really help the coast guard very much."

■ WHILE RUM-RUNNERS ON THE PACIFIC Coast worked directly from Canada, on the Atlantic side of the continent they used convenient foreign ports where alcohol could be received for transshipment into the US. The Bahamas, Cuba, British Honduras (Belize) and Bermuda all served as conduits for booze from Britain and Canada. Nassau, the capital of the Bahamas, boomed in the early years of prohibition. Daniel Okrent points out that in the two years before America went dry, 914 gallons of Scotch entered the Bahamas; by 1922 that amount had jumped to 386,000 gallons. Another

A collection of postcards that emphasize the grave (pun intended) dangers of alcohol. The warning is clear: an early death awaits the heavy drinker. The card on the top right maps the course of the road much travelled from the innocence of a glass of lemonade through highballs and whisky to the dreaded absinthe and an alcohol-assisted demise. The verse on the bottom card is an irreverent parody of a popular nineteenth-century sentimental poem, "Little Jim (The Collier's Dying Child)" by Edward Farmer. The original lines were: "I have no pain, dear mother, now / But oh! I am so dry; / Just moisten poor Jim's lips again, / And, mother, don't you cry."

LEFT Crew of a rum-running vessel shows off some of their cargo. The man second from left is holding several bottles of rye wrapped in burlap. Known as a "burlock," or "sack," this was a favourite way to pack liquor bottles for easy handling.

BELOW Longshoremen load cases of Canadian Club whisky onto a rum-running schooner on the Nassau waterfront in 1924. The Bahamian port was an important transshipment centre in the early years of American prohibition.

historian estimates that as much as ten million quarts of liquor passed through Nassau in a year. Of course, so much liquor was not meant for Bahamians. As quickly as it could be transferred to the rum-running vessels it was on its way again, up the coast to "Rum Row," the off-shore marketplace between Boston and Atlantic City.

Rum Row was said to be the invention of a former merchant mariner named Bill McCoy. In 1921 McCoy acquired a 90-foot (27.4-metre) fishing schooner, loaded it with 1,500 cases of whisky he acquired in Nassau and sailed to the coast of Georgia where he sold the entire shipment. A few weeks later McCoy returned with another load, this time to the vicinity of New York where he waited offshore for word to spread among the bootleggers that he had arrived and was open for business. So successful was this venture that he upgraded to a larger vessel, the 114-foot (34.5-metre), two-masted schooner *Tomoka,* capable of handling 5,000 cases at a time. McCoy is credited with another invention adopted by the rum-running fleet: the "burlock." Smugglers commonly removed bottles of alcohol from their wooden crates and repacked them in burlap sacks for ease of handling. McCoy's innovation was to take six bottles, surround them in a protective jacket of straw in the shape of a pyramid, then wrap the whole package tightly in burlap. The result, known also as a "sack," made economical use of stowage space and could be handed over the gunwales with ease.

At this time the Coast Guard was not yet a serious impediment to business and the atmosphere on Rum Row was relaxed and friendly with customers coming out in all manner of boats to make their purchases. Boaters out for a day cruise might arrive just to buy a bottle or two for personal consumption and there were reports of rum vessels hanging price lists over the side like vegetable vendors at an open-air market. One enterprising yacht owner hired a band, put some waiters in uniform and established a floating speakeasy just beyond the three-mile limit. Eventually this maritime shopping mall evolved into a more permanent fleet of large vessels, floating warehouses that remained off the coast more or less permanently, careful to stay beyond the three-mile territorial limit, while smaller vessels re-supplied them from Nassau and the other ports.

Rye whisky packed in burlap sacks is stowed in the hold of an Atlantic rum-runner, possibly the *Tomoka,* docked at Nassau. Prohibition was a windfall for the Bahamas, at the time a British colony. The local government used the small export tax it imposed on the rum-runners to finance all kinds of public improvements.

Bill McCoy takes machine-gun practice aboard the *Tomoka*. When he was captured by the Coast Guard in November 1923 the gun was actually used as McCoy attempted to make his escape, but when the Coast Guard vessel *Seneca* lofted a few well-aimed shells into the water beside him McCoy surrendered. Violent encounters with the law became ever more common as the decade wore on.

In 1922 another seaport opened to the rum-running trade. The tiny island of Saint-Pierre and its neighbour Miquelon, anchored in the North Atlantic just south of Newfoundland, had been claimed for France in 1536 by the explorer Jacques Cartier. Over the years, ownership of the sparsely populated islands had bounced back and forth between France and Britain as the spoils of their colonial wars until finally the Treaty of Paris in 1814 left them in French hands for good. Following World War I the government in Paris had banned the importation of alcohol into all its overseas possessions, including Saint-Pierre and Miquelon, as a way of preserving foreign exchange, but in April 1922 Paris lifted the ban and the islands, located so conveniently close to the Eastern Seaboard, were set to become the liquor entrepôt of the North Atlantic.

Once again it is Bill McCoy who gets credit for recognizing the extra-legal possibilities of Saint-Pierre. As the story goes, in the spring of 1922 his vessel *Tomoka*, dodging the authorities and in need of repairs, was waiting off Halifax for permission to enter the harbour. Because the schooner had on board a shipment of liquor from

Nassau, permission was denied. A frustrated McCoy, who had come to Halifax to meet his vessel, fell into conversation with a merchant from Saint-Pierre named Folquet who was staying at the same hotel. When Folquet learned of the rum-runner's predicament he offered not only to fix the boat but to act as McCoy's agent on Saint-Pierre, an island the American did not even know existed. Once McCoy paid his first visit, he recognized immediately that he'd found a perfect place to do business. The writer Damon Runyon called Saint-Pierre "a little squirt of a burg." Prior to prohibition it served mainly as a port of call for the French fishing fleet. Its population of fewer than four thousand inhabitants was in decline as the exodus that had begun during the war continued for lack of economic opportunities. In this situation the rum-runners were welcome when they came offering jobs, incomes and adventure to a population hungry for all three. It was not long before Saint-Pierre was challenging the southern ports for pre-eminence in the Eastern Seaboard liquor business. (The Bahamas and Havana remained the main suppliers to Florida and the Gulf of Mexico.)

K. 53.

BOTTLING LABEL
ACCOUNT OF
SPIRITS EXPORTED IN CASES

INLAND REVENUE

Licensed distillers were required by law to keep records of all their exports. This 1921 account book belonged to the Seagram company and records exports to Brazil, the Bahamas, England and Norway, among other places. Much of this liquor would have found its way back into the US. Joseph Seagram (1841–1919) was a grist mill manager, then mill owner, in Waterloo, Ontario. During the 1880s he expanded the distilling side of the business and was soon exporting to the US and Britain. In 1911 the operation was incorporated as Joseph E. Seagram and Sons Ltd. His signature product was rye whisky, Seagram's 83 and later Seagram's V.O. Every barrel used in the distillery was identified as belonging to the company with the use of this stencil attached to the barrel heads. Following Joseph's death one of his sons took over the business; it was sold in 1928 to the Bronfmans.

BELOW The French islands of Saint-Pierre and Miquelon became transshipment centres where liquor was collected perfectly legally, then transferred to boats and shipped not so legally into the Eastern US. Here, crates of booze are being moved by sleigh from warehouses in Saint-Pierre to ships docked in the harbour.

RIGHT The port of Saint-Pierre boomed during the prohibition era as almost every resident of the island found work of some kind in the rum-running business.

Within a year the Saint-Pierre waterfront was transformed into a bustling metropolis with cargoes of Scotch arriving from Scotland, Irish whiskey from Ireland, champagne from France, rum from Demerara, and rye and bourbon from Canada. While vessels waited to take on a load their crews took advantage of the several bars on shore to drink and gamble. The demand for warehouse space soon outstripped the supply and every available building on the island was commandeered for storage. So many jobs were available loading and unloading the crates of liquor and working on the launches that carried the booze down to Rum Row that the locals abandoned the fishery altogether. Eventually the fish-packing plant had to close; it became a liquor storehouse instead. In 1923 more than a thousand vessels left Saint-Pierre for Rum Row carrying six million bottles of hooch.

Most of the large liquor dealers from Canada established warehouses in Saint-Pierre. Consolidated Exporters, for example, represented United Distillers, a prominent Vancouver distillery. Consolidated Traders did business for the Montreal liquor giant Canadian Industrial Alcohol Ltd., owner of Corby's. Another agency, the Great West Wine Company, represented the Reifel interests in Saint-Pierre. The Bronfmans had their own subsidiary as well, the Northern Export Company, which grew to become the largest trader on the island; at one point there were seventy people working at the Northern Export warehouse and office in Saint-Pierre. As time went on, a few Canadian distillers came to handle most of the liquor that moved in and out of the island port. One reason that the liquor merchants appreciated Saint-Pierre was that the French imposed only a four-cent-per-bottle tax, less than fifty cents per case, much lower than the six dollars per case exporters had to pay in the Bahamas. For Canadian dealers, Saint-Pierre also was convenient because they did not have to go through the charade of finagling the customs documents. Shippers from Canada, such as the Bronfmans, Gooderham & Worts and Hiram Walker, were required to put up a bond equal to double the cash value of a shipment, refundable when proof was provided that the shipment had reached its declared destination of Cuba, Nassau, or wherever. The easiest way of getting around this requirement was to send the paperwork

The Coast Guard cutter *Dexter* was one of thirteen patrol boats built during 1925–26 by Defoe Boat and Motor Works of Bay City, Michigan, for use against the rumrunners in the Great Lakes and on the East Coast.

The *Dexter* was one of the Coast Guard vessels that chased down the *I'm Alone* in the Gulf of Mexico in 1929. It is now part of an artificial reef at the bottom of Lake Michigan near Chicago.

to an agent in the destination port who had been bribed to confirm that, yes, the shipment had arrived. When the signed documents arrived back in Canada the shipper got the bond payment back and the liquor went on its way into the US pipeline. Now Canadian shipments could simply be exported to nearby Saint-Pierre, receive all the legitimate signatures and customs stamps that freed up the deposits, and be rerouted down to Rum Row.

■ INITIALLY THE US COAST GUARD FLEET of patrol vessels was small and understaffed. If a rum vessel was caught it was more by accident than design. The Coast Guard was like a small flea annoying a very large dog but not inflicting real pain. The agency itself estimated that it was intercepting just five percent of the liquor entering the US by sea. As on the West Coast, Atlantic rum-runners had more to fear from pirates and hijackers than they did from the government. The occasional body washing ashore gave evidence of violent confrontations taking place at sea, the details of which were sometimes never known. One gruesome incident near Martha's Vineyard in 1923 signalled that the carefree days were over. The mutilated

corpses of eight crew members of the steam trawler *John Dwight,* which was carrying a cargo of Canadian beer, were found floating in the water near the Vineyard. The men had been tortured before their bodies were tossed into the sea. For all its aura of adventure and derring-do, rum-running was a deadly serious business.

To reduce the amount of money that was changing hands, and thereby attracting visits from sea-going thieves, the crime syndicates who controlled the liquor traffic worked out a fulfillment system that required no cash. When orders were placed and paid for, a customer received half of a torn dollar bill or a torn playing card. The other half was sent to the rum vessel. When a shore boat arrived to pick up an order the customer's torn half of the bill had to be shown, sometimes with the order written on it, before the liquor was released.

In the mid-1920s the Coast Guard received a huge infusion of $14 million from the treasury to upgrade and expand its operations. More than three hundred new vessels were added to the fleet – cutters, cabin cruisers, speedboats – along with hundreds of new officers. Most of the craft came

equipped with shortwave radio. The Coast Guard became much more aggressive about stopping the rum navy. Combined with the extension of the territorial limit to 12 miles (19 kilometres), this strengthening of the Coast Guard marked a turning of the tide in the fight against the rum-runners but also an increase in the level of violence at sea.

One notorious Canadian victim of this get-tough approach was the *I'm Alone*, a 125-foot (38-metre) fishing schooner built in Lunenburg, Nova Scotia, that cruised regularly between Saint-Pierre and Rum Row. During the summer the *I'm Alone* worked in tandem with a high-powered tender, the No. 174. Equipped with four aircraft engines, the No. 174 was able to outrun the US Coast Guard as it ferried liquor back and forth between the schooner and the mainland. During the winter of 1928-29, under new ownership and with a new skipper, the *I'm Alone* shifted its area of operation south to the Gulf of Mexico. In March 1929 two Coast Guard cutters managed to chase down the *I'm Alone* in the Gulf loaded with a cargo of whisky and rum from Belize. Certain that his boat was outside the territorial limit and safe from US

BELOW **US Customs** patrol boats head out on the Detroit River to hunt for rum-runners. By the early 1930s, when this photograph was taken, the American authorities had stepped up their patrols throughout the Great Lakes region.

RIGHT **The US Coast** Guard launched a small navy of vessels to stem the flow of liquor from Canada, among them this new patrol boat, designed to chase down the speedy rum-runners on the Detroit River.

LEFT **US Coast Guard 8031** began life as a speedy rum-running vessel. Seized by the Coast Guard, it was put right back to work chasing smugglers on behalf of the government. Built for speed, streamlined and low in the water, the boat is a perfect example of the type of launch that ferried liquor from Rum Row into shore.

OPPOSITE **The crew of the Canadian schooner *I'm Alone* languishes in an American jail after the rum-runner was chased down and sunk by the US Coast Guard in the Gulf of Mexico in March 1929. One crewman died and the affair caused a diplomatic incident. Eventually an international court ruled that the US was at fault and ordered restitution.**

THE CUSTOMS PREVENTIVE SERVICE

■ The Canadian equivalent of the US Coast Guard was the Customs Preventive Service (CPS). Since 1892 a single vessel belonging to the Service had patrolled the Atlantic coast to interdict smugglers, occasionally assisted by fisheries patrol vessels. With the arrival of prohibition, and the concern about rum-runners diverting some of their cargo back into Canada, the federal government funded a modest expansion of the CPS fleet on the East Coast to eight vessels by 1924, though most of them were too slow to be of much use combating the rum-runners.

It was the customs scandal of 1926–27 that breathed real life into the Service. From then on the strength of its fleet increased steadily, reflecting the government's new determination to stop liquor smuggling. By the end of the decade the Service had thirty vessels and a budget of a million dollars.

In 1932 the CPS was absorbed into the RCMP Marine Section and disappeared as a separate entity.

prosecution, Captain Jack Randell refused to stop. The Coast Guard vessels, however, insisted they had the law on their side. They opened fire with artillery and rifles, wounding Randell in the thigh and eventually sinking the *I'm Alone*. One member of the crew died. The incident sparked international outrage (the dead sailor was French; the boat was Canadian) against the high-handedness of the US Coast Guard. It was either an act of war or an act of piracy, claimed one Canadian Member of Parliament. Either way it added fuel to the diplomatic fire that had already been stoked by similar incidents on the Great Lakes. The matter was finally resolved in 1935 when an international commission ordered the US to apologize and pay $50,666 to the Canadian government plus another $25,666 to Captain Randell and his crew.

In response to the Coast Guard's expansion of its fleet, the smugglers also upgraded, building new types of speedboats that could outrun even the fastest Coast Guard vessel. Among these were the "banana boats," most of which were built in Lunenburg, Nova Scotia. Banana boats all followed the same design: narrow, low-slung, with a flattish bottom; in other words, a shape resembling

a banana. The intention was to make them as hard as possible to spot on the water. Equipped with a pair of powerful engines and capable of carrying several thousand cases of liquor, the so-called "Banana Fleet" ran between Saint-Pierre and the coastal US, often slipping directly into New York harbour under cover of darkness. Their origins in Lunenburg came as no surprise; it has been estimated that at least half the town's fishing fleet turned to rum-running during the 1920s.

Hugh Corkum was a crewman aboard one of the banana boats. Corkum had joined the rum-runners as a fifteen-year-old to support his family in Lunenburg. His first trip had been aboard the *W.H. Eastwood*, a four-masted, 153-foot (46.6-metre) schooner. The *Eastwood* left Halifax in the dead of winter 1927 and headed for Saint-Pierre. Along with twelve thousand cases of assorted liquor, Corkum reported, the *Eastwood* welcomed aboard an American "gangster-style supercargo" whose job it was to protect the booze for its owner. This desperado, who was drunk for most of the voyage, strolled around the decks wearing a revolver in his belt and shouting threats at the crew.

THE RUM-RUNNERS • 151

Radio communication was central to the success of the rum-running enterprise. A ship needed to send and receive instructions about where a rendezvous was going to take place. Because the Coast Guard was listening in, these communications had to be in code. This is a page from a radio operator's code book. When the authorities seized a rum-running vessel, the code book was the first thing the crew tossed overboard so as not to give away incriminating information.

```
MONDAY                    BOAT # 3
BOAT-TO-SHORE = CRD
SHORE-TO-BOAT = M7
        TUESDAY
BOAT  TO  SHORE = DAS
SHORE  TO  BOAT = CM
        WEDNESDAY
BOAT  TO  SHORE = JOY
SHORE  TO  BOAT = OH
        THURSDAY
BOAT  TO  SHORE = LVI
SHORE  TO  BOAT = 6Y
        FRIDAY
BOAT  TO  SHORE = XYZ
SHORE  TO  BOAT = SU
        SATURDAY
BOAT  TO  SHORE = PIZ
SHORE  TO  BOAT = 09
        SUNDAY
BOAT  TO  SHORE = BVD
SHORE  TO  BOAT = AF
```

A shore boat makes contact with the schooner *Katherine* off the coast of New Jersey in 1923 to smuggle a load of liquor ashore.

At length the captain, who himself was drunk at the time, settled things by punching the supercargo in the stomach with a bottle of whisky, breaking three of his ribs and putting him on his back for the rest of the trip. The *Eastwood* was supposed to off-load its cargo in Buzzard's Bay, Massachusetts, but it was spotted by a pair of Coast Guard cutters, which foiled all attempts to rendezvous with any shore boats and the would-be smugglers had to return to Saint-Pierre without delivering a single case. It was an unsatisfying start for young Corkum but he had better luck when he joined the Banana Fleet early in 1928, at least for a while.

The *Harbour Trader* was almost 140 feet (43 metres) long with a nine-person crew and a capacity of 4,600 cases. Corkum called it the "Queen of the Banana Fleet." The *Trader*'s home base was Liverpool, Nova Scotia, where it returned after every trip for refuelling and a refit. As Corkum explained in his memoirs, jobs on the banana boats were much sought after by the young seamen of Nova Scotia's South Shore. "All our crew were respectable family men of good character," said Corkum, "who had no feelings of guilt about what they were doing. They felt

they were doing a job which gave them the opportunity to make a much better living than they could make fishing, freighting, or by their other previous occupations." Corkum, for example, received $75 per month along with a bonus of $150 "for every trip successfully landed ... This was big money in 1928."

On average the vessel made one voyage a month between Saint-Pierre and the New York area, lasting about two weeks. Invariably there was a supercargo aboard, an American named Max Holtz who took care of the money side of things. Holtz "was always immaculately groomed and dressed," Corkum recalled, and used to shine his binoculars with a hundred-dollar bill. The *Trader* followed a consistent pattern. Cruising well off-shore to avoid the Coast Guard cutters, it waited to receive a radio message telling it where and when to make a drop. Deliveries were always made on a moonless night. Sometimes the vessel motored right up next to a wharf; at other times it was met close to shore by a small flotilla of speedboats that took away the cargo. Always it had to play cat and mouse with the patrol boats in the dark, avoiding the bright searchlights that

probed the water. It was tense work and the men did it knowing that sooner or later they would probably get caught. For Corkum that moment came at the end of 1928 on his twelfth trip. The *Trader* was in the middle of transferring its cargo somewhere in the middle of New York Bay when Holtz sounded the alarm. The closely guarded secret of their position had been leaked by an informant. The shore boats evaporated into the night and the *Trader* made a run for it but it was overtaken by a cutter that threatened to blow it out of the water. As the Coast Guard boarded one side of the boat the wireless operator was throwing his code book and other incriminating documents into the water on the other side. Then the crew sat down and toasted their capture with a drink.

Corkum might have thought he was in for some jail time but that was not how things worked. Whomever he was hauling booze for provided the captain with money to cover all expenses for the crew while they were in New York. For six weeks Corkum stayed in a comfortable hotel near Times Square, dining out every night, hitting the nightspots and seeing the sights. Finally he and the others were handed railway tickets and

Customers flock to a Detroit liquor store in the days before prohibition was declared in the US in January 1920. The sign reads: "The Last Call – The time is getting shorter and so is our stock. Buy now or you'll be without it bye and bye. We carry the most complete high grade liquors in the city." It was the beginning of one of the most daring social experiments in Canadian and US history, and led to an era of widespread corruption and popular lawlessness.

told they could go home. They never even saw the inside of a courtroom. The *Trader* was less fortunate: it was declared forfeit and handed over to the Coast Guard which used it as a harbour patrol boat for several years. Meanwhile Corkum, undiscouraged, returned to the life of the rum-runner.

■ WITH THE END OF PROHIBITION IN THE US, most of the rum-runners went back to making a living on the right side of the law. Johnny Schnarr took up commercial fishing. Hugh Corkum became a police officer. Fraser Miles went to college and became an electrical engineer. Captain Charles Hudson sold yachts. And almost universally they recalled their years as maritime smugglers without regret and without apology. "Sure, it was illegal as far as the Americans were concerned," Schnarr admitted, "but that never bothered me too much. I couldn't see where I was doing anything terribly wrong." What he liked about the work was the adventure and the challenge. "In looking back on it, I'd have to say that that challenge of staying out of reach of the authorities meant as much to me as anything else. I certainly wasn't in the business just for the money.

I could have made a lot more money than I did, if that was my prime motivation." He loved working on the water and even as the bullets flew he loved playing hide and seek with the Coast Guard. It was, he concluded, the most exciting time of his life.

If the rum-runners found the work exciting, the big distillery cartels found it hugely profitable. True, some of them were hauled into court when it was all over and had to pay fairly substantial amounts in fines and back taxes. But the amounts were minuscule compared to the profits they made during prohibition, all condoned by a federal government that preferred to turn a blind eye to what was going on. For everyone involved – producers, suppliers, consumers, regulators – rum-running represented the most dramatic incidence of popular lawlessness in the country's history.

With the exception of Scandinavia, where Iceland, Norway and Finland all banned alcohol during and after World War I, prohibition did not have the same acceptance in Europe as it did in North America. Europeans generally were more tolerant of liquor consumption and even when they weren't they were reluctant to control it through legislation. While North Americans were experimenting with prohibition, Europeans were experimenting with avant-garde artistic movements like Fauvism and Cubism. One of the earliest exponents of Cubism was Juan Gris (1887–1927), a Spanish-born painter who spent most of his working life in France where he was a friend of Pablo Picasso and Georges Braque, the acknowledged founders of the movement. Gris completed this Cubist canvas, "Still Life with Bordeaux Bottle," in 1919, the year of his first major solo exhibition in Paris. It shows his characteristic use of overlapping flat planes of shape and colour.

CHAPTER FIVE

Foreign Vessels Now Carry Our Tourist Trade ALL GETTING AMERICA DOLLARS

PROHIBITION Is Ruining Our Merchant Marine 600 AMERICAN VESSELS ARE TIED TO THE DOCKS

4,000,000 AMERICAN SOLDIER FOUGHT FOR LIBERT AND WERE REWARD WITH PROHIBITIO HOW COME ?

TO C YOU CR O CA

I'm gonna leave this town, everything is closin' down…
I'm leavin' in the summer, and I won't be back 'til fall.
Goodbye Broadway, Hello Montreal.

– Lyric from "Hello Montreal" as sung by TED LEWIS, 1928

HELLO NEIGHBOUR, LET'S HAVE A DRINK

■ THE DECADE OF THE 1920s WAS A period of burgeoning tourism in Canada, especially from the United States. Of course, vacationing Americans had been coming north for years, attracted by the romanticism of Old Quebec, the majesty of Niagara Falls, the rugged grandeur of the Rocky Mountains, the exoticism of the First Nations and the beauty of the northern landscape. Prohibition, however, added one more reason, and a compelling one, for American tourists to come to Canada, a travel destination that was close, comfortably familiar yet still faintly exotic, and best of all, wet. Many of these visitors arrived by automobile. During the 1920s car ownership was expanding rapidly on both sides of the border. The number of registered vehicles in the US rose from eight million to twenty-three million during the decade. By 1925 two million American-owned motor cars were entering Canada annually, many of their owners attracted by the lack of prohibition in most of the provinces. The historian of American prohibition, Daniel Okrent, estimates that

by the end of the decade liquor tourists were spending $300 million a year in Canada. The Depression slowed this northward flow but certainly did not end it; in 1933, the final year of prohibition in the US, seven million American tourists entered Ontario alone. Much infrastructure was built to accommodate these visitors: roads, bridges, parks, campsites, motels ... and drinking spots. These watering holes ranged from makeshift farmhouse "taverns" located close to the border to palatial hotels and Jazz Age urban nightclubs. Whatever the style of establishment or the class of customer, by the middle of the '20s Canada had flung its doors wide to thirsty Americans.

■ ON THE PACIFIC COAST, ONE OF THE entertainment meccas built to attract Americans frustrated by prohibition in neighbouring Washington State was the Peace Portal golf course, developed by promoter Sam Hill. A graduate of Harvard University, Hill was a corporate lawyer and a senior executive with the Great Northern Railway,

The Pacific Highway, opened in July 1913, connected New Westminster, British Columbia, to the border at Blaine, Washington. Paved in 1923, the highway carried a multitude of American motorists north to take advantage of BC's more liberal drinking laws.

the American transcontinental line that arrived in Seattle in 1893. Having moved to the Pacific Northwest along with the railway, Hill became an enthusiastic proponent of highway building to accommodate the Model Ts and other motor vehicles that were just beginning to take to the road. In concert with Alfred Todd, a former mayor of Victoria and a motor-car enthusiast himself, Hill came up with the idea for a monument to peace to be constructed where the Pacific Highway crossed the border near Blaine. Opened in 1921, the Peace Arch commemorates amicable relations between Canada and the US. On a more personal note, Hill wanted a place where he could entertain his friends and business associates without the inconvenience of prohibition; in other words, north of the border in Canada. He decided to build a resort, called the Semiahmoo Club, which included a golf course, a restaurant and a hotel. As well, Hill constructed a summer home on the site for himself and his family. The restaurant/bar side of the operation opened in 1927; the first nine holes of the proposed eighteen-hole golf course followed in September 1929. Hill died before his vision for the property was

fully realized but under the direction of his cousin Edgar Hill the golf course, renamed Peace Portal Golf Club, was fully operational by the summer of 1932 and remains in business today.

If building a golf course seems like an extravagant way to get a drink, it was a modest venture compared to the Prince of Wales Hotel in Waterton, Alberta. The Prince of Wales was conceived by another American railway executive, Louis Hill (no relation to Sam) principally to appeal to an American clientele and once again the Great Northern Railway (GNR) was involved. Louis was the son of the renowned transportation tycoon James J. Hill, the financier behind the construction of the Great Northern. Louis had joined the railway as a young man and by 1912, at age forty, he was chairman of the board. The GNR had spurred efforts to create Glacier National Park in northern Montana, where it invested heavily in tourist facilities, and when Alberta abandoned its own experiment with prohibition in 1924 Hill recognized the tourism potential of a hotel, with a bar, in Waterton Lakes National Park just across the border from Glacier Park. On March 5, 1926, the *New York World*

A large crowd turns out to witness the official opening of the Peace Arch at the border near Blaine, Washington, in September 1921. The Arch commemorates a history of peaceable relations between the US and Canada. On the American side an inscription reads "Children of a common mother" while on the Canadian side the inscription is "Brethren dwelling together in unity."

newspaper reported that "the Great Northern will build a haven for thirsty American travellers at Waterton, Alberta..." The new hotel would sit atop a hill overlooking Upper Waterton Lake with a sweeping view south down the lake into Montana. The railway was reluctant to advertise its plans for a beer parlour for fear of arousing local opposition – Waterton was not far from Cardston, home to a sizeable population of teetotalling Mormons – but it lobbied successfully behind the scenes to obtain a liquor licence and two weeks after the ninety-room Prince of Wales Hotel welcomed its first customers in July 1927, so did the beer parlour. The bar served only beer but spirits could be ordered from the bellman and brought in from Lethbridge on the hotel supply truck. In design, the Prince of Wales, which is still in operation, evokes the chateau style of the famous Canadian railway hotels – the Banff Springs, the Château Laurier in Ottawa, and the Château Frontenac in Quebec City, to name just three. When it opened it boasted all the mod cons, including an elevator, hot and cold running water, bathtubs in every room, a barbershop, even a dispensary with its own resident nurse. American customers were

ferried north from Glacier Park by road in jitneys and touring cars provided by the Great Northern, and by boat up the lake aboard the company's sleek launch, MV *International*.

In the summer of 1932 the *International* began a reverse excursion from Waterton that provided one of the most popular entertainment options in southern Alberta. It also highlighted the difficulty of enforcing liquor laws when no one wanted to obey them. In this case it was Canadians setting out on Sunday afternoons aboard the *International* to cruise south down the lake to Goat Haunt, Montana, where the GNR had built a small dance pavilion. Well-known Canadian musician Mart Kenney and his band, the Western Gentlemen, who were performing the rest of the week in Waterton, provided the music and the railway provided the beer. (Revellers who wanted something stronger brought their own.) On Sundays it was illegal to purchase drink in Alberta, and until the end of 1933 it was illegal to drink any day of the week in the US, but who was paying attention in this out-of-the-way wilderness dance pavilion? These so-called "midnight frolics" continued on the deck of the *International* all the way back to Waterton

■ Of all the reminders of the prohibition era that still exist perhaps none is as curious as the underground tunnels in Moose Jaw, Saskatchewan. Originally built for the steam heating system that served many of the downtown buildings, the tunnels later were occupied by Chinese immigrants, many of whom had come to the Canadian West to work on the construction of the transcontinental railway. Suffering poverty and racism, some of these families sought refuge in the tunnels where they made makeshift homes for themselves, emerging by day to work in laundries, restaurants, burlap bag factories, and at odd jobs.

Once prohibition arrived, Moose Jaw took advantage of its location as a rail hub and the tunnels were used to store liquor and organize clandestine shipments to Chicago and other places in the US. Local legend says that many mobsters came to town to buy booze for their bootleg operations, including Al Capone and Diamond Jim Brady. Today the tunnels are one of Saskatchewan's main tourist attractions.

A postcard shows the Huntingdon Chateau in Huntingdon, Quebec, near the border with New York State southwest of Montreal, one of several rural hotels across Canada that had bars catering to American visitors.

where the band was usually still playing when the boat docked in the wee hours of the morning.

On the other side of the country, in southern Quebec, hotel owners were also welcoming an influx of American visitors. (In this they were no different from the hoteliers around Windsor, Ontario, whose roadhouses hosted Americans arriving across the Detroit River by boat.) In the small community of Huntingdon, Quebec, for example – southwest of Montreal close to the border with New York State – business at the Moir Hotel was so good that its owner decided to replace it with a larger establishment. Huntingdon was situated on a well-used liquor-smuggling route between Montreal and upstate New York and the county saw its fair share of excitement during prohibition. "Smugglers infest the northern border," admitted one New York judge. Farms on the Canadian side were used to store shipments of booze headed for the US, and armed enforcement officers patrolled the roads at night in high-powered cars looking for smugglers. "It was dangerous to be on the road at night," recalled a local resident, "for there were hijackers on the

road, and the patrol men did not hesitate to shoot at anyone who refused to stop." In Huntingdon itself the new hotel catered not to smugglers but to legitimate travellers attracted by Quebec's relaxed liquor regulations. The three-storey Huntingdon Chateau, which opened for business in November 1929 (ironically, just a few weeks after the New York stock market crash signalled the beginning of the Great Depression), was one of the finest hotels anywhere in rural Canada with a large ballroom as well as a dining room and a kitchen managed by a professional chef. And of course a cocktail lounge with its own ten-piece orchestra playing from Easter to Thanksgiving where Americans would come to dine and dance in a bibulous atmosphere. Even with the onset of the Depression the hotel managed to turn an annual profit, though it was perhaps no coincidence that once American prohibition was repealed business at the hotel declined and cost-saving measures had to be introduced.

■ OF SPECIAL INTEREST TO "LIQUOR tourists" from the US were urban nightspots featuring the new jazz music that was filtering north from New Orleans and black

communities in the South. In 1917 the United States was swept up in a "jazz craze," sparked by the first recordings of the new music, and this enthusiasm among young people for the new sound and the scandalizing dance forms that went with it spilled across the border into Canada. As usual, what the younger generation embraced, the older generation feared. "Jazz disorganizes all regular laws and order," a writer in *Maclean's* magazine warned in 1921; "it stimulates to extreme deeds, to a breaking away from all rules and conventions; it is harmful and dangerous, and its influence is wholly bad."

In Vancouver, American jazz musicians came to play at hotels and bars, especially those catering to the city's own black population which was concentrated in the eastside Strathcona neighbourhood. The most popular joint was the Patricia Hotel on East Hastings Street where Will Bowman managed the Patricia Café. By the middle of 1920 one American paper was reporting: "Word comes from Vancouver, B.C., that Bill Bowman's Patricia Café is the talk of the town." The reporter went on to acknowledge that American prohibition had something

MONTMARTRE

59 ST. CATHERINE OUEST

NOUVELLE REVUE ET

Mynie Suttons Swing Orchestre

DE COULEUR DIRECTEMENT
DE HARLEM NEW YORK

Danse × Repas Biere × Vin

A. Allard Prop   Reservation PL. 7368   W. Légaré Gérant

MONTMARTRE

59 ST. CATHERINE WEST

A NEW SPARKLING RED-HOT
HARLEM COLOURED REVUE

INCLUDING

Mynie Suttons Swing Orchestra

DANCE - DINE   Reservation   BEER - WINE

A. Allard Prop.   PLateau 7368   Harry Miller H. W.

"WHERE MONTREAL STEPS OUT"

MONTMARTRE CABARET

— 59 ST. CATHERINE ST. WEST —

The Show Place Featuring Colored Stars,
World Famous Harlem Blue Singers and
Torrid Dancers Carefree and Happy —
With

"Put 'A' Top On It"

Johnny Gardner

As Master of Ceremonies
in "THE SHOW BOAT REVUE"

MYNIE SUTTON   And His Rhythm Montmartiers
Swinging Out.

DANCE   RES. PL. 0043-7368   BEER
DINE   Southern Fried Chicken a Specialty by   WINE
Our Colored Chef.

These are advertising cards for the Montmartre Cabaret on St. Catherine Street West, "where Montreal steps out." Prohibition-era cabarets in the city featured burlesque and vaudeville performers and most of the leading jazz musicians of the period, including Ontario's own Myron "Mynie" Sutton and his swing orchestra. (One of Sutton's original compositions was titled "Moanin' at the Montmartre.") The advertisements promise an experience akin to a Harlem nightclub or a Parisian café. Mynie Sutton began piano lessons in his native Niagara Falls when he was nine years old and later learned the clarinet and alto saxophone as well. As a teenager he played in area dance bands and then turned professional.

In 1931 he formed a six-piece group called the Canadian Ambassadors in Guelph. Two years later the band moved to Montreal where for the next six years it headlined at many of the city's nightspots. With its lax liquor laws and proximity to the US, Montreal was known as a swinging, wide-open city during the prohibition era.

Ada "Bricktop" Smith began touring on the vaudeville circuit when she was a teenager. In the early 1920s she appeared along with Jelly Roll Morton in Vancouver jazz clubs before both went on to achieve fame elsewhere. Bricktop travelled to Paris where she opened her own club, Chez Bricktop's, in 1926. Until the onset of World War II forced her return to the US, Bricktop's was at the centre of the Parisian nightclub scene.

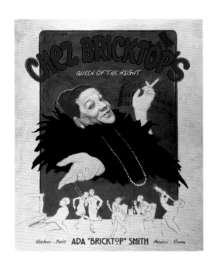

to do with it. "That's a country where you can 'crook your elbow' and never be molested," he wrote. This was not entirely accurate since BC had its own prohibition until 1923, but hotel owners got around the law by establishing private clubs where patrons could legally consume liquor that they brought with them. In 1919 Bowman had introduced a 28-year-old itinerant pianist named Jelly Roll Morton to Vancouver jazz lovers. Morton, then balancing on the cusp of stardom, played at the Patricia and other clubs around town before departing in 1922 for the bright lights of Chicago and eventual fame as one of the pre-eminent jazz pianists and composers of the era. Also performing at the Patricia was the African-American dancer and singer Ada "Bricktop" Smith. A native of West Virginia, Bricktop got her nickname from the bright red hair she inherited from her Irish father. She would go on to open a celebrated nightclub in the Rue Pigalle in Paris frequented by Jazz Age celebrities like Cole Porter and F. Scott Fitzgerald, but her Vancouver years were decidedly less flamboyant. The Patricia was the kind of rough-and-tumble nightspot that one would expect to find in a port city

not far removed from the frontier. Bricktop had a leg broken during one brawl and in her memoirs she particularly singled out the thick-necked Swedish loggers who descended on Vancouver from the coastal camps and "could make a bottle of whiskey disappear in no time." Vancouver was officially a "dry town," Bricktop observed, but liquor flowed freely at clubs, speakeasies and private parties. This combination of relaxed liquor enforcement and hot jazz attracted a steady flow of American visitors to the city's clubs and dance halls.

But it was Montreal that gained a reputation with Americans for being a wide-open city where visitors were able to indulge a passion for the "Three Ds": dancing, dining and drinking. Quebec had not embraced prohibition to the same degree as other provinces, introducing it in a modified form at the end of the war and even then only briefly. As a result, Montreal was the most uninhibited big city on the continent when it came to its liquor laws and the nightlife they encouraged. "Alcohol oils the gears of the nightclub industry and pays the salaries of its workers," Montreal jazz historian John Gilmore has written, "and in Montreal alcohol flowed

No writer expressed the youthful energy and hedonism of the "Jazz Age" (a term he invented) more than F. Scott Fitzgerald. When his first novel, *This Side of Paradise*, appeared in 1920 it scandalized the American public with its portrait of a younger generation in revolt against the old moral standards. Women, who were supposed to be the guardians of morality, were smoking cigarettes and drinking gin, wearing scandalously short skirts and flinging themselves shamelessly around the dance floor to the rhythms of the new up-tempo music. Two years later both his second novel, *The Beautiful and the Damned*, and this collection of stories, *Tales of the Jazz Age*, were published. They solidified Fitzgerald's reputation as the voice of a new generation.

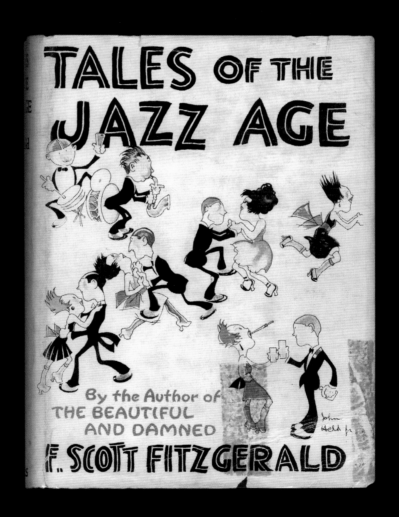

HELLO MONTREAL

■ THE SWINGING 1928 TUNE "Hello Montreal" conveys the sense of Montreal being a prohibition-era mecca for jazz musicians and the people who liked to listen to them.

The tune was made popular by Ted Lewis, a clarinet player and band leader who was known as "Mr. Entertainment." Not a particularly original musician himself, his band included legendary jazz names like Muggsy Spanier and Benny Goodman and was one of the leading jazz ensembles of the 1920s, both live and on record. Lewis was known for his battered top hat and his familiar catch-phrase, "Is everybody happy?"

Speak easy, speak easy, said Johnny Brown,
Why I'm gonna leave this town, everything is closin' down.
Speak easy, speak easy, and tell the bunch,
I won't go east, I won't go west, I've got a different hunch.
I'm leavin' in the summer, and I won't be back 'til fall.
Goodbye Broadway, Hello Montreal.

With a stein upon the table, I'll be laughing at you all.
Goodbye Broadway, Hello Montreal.
That old tin pail, that old tin pail,
You know that pail was never meant to carry ginger ale.
And if my wife wants me, you can tell her where to call,
It's goodbye Broadway, hello Montreal.

With lyrics by Billy Rose and Mort Dixon and music by Harry Warren, "Hello Montreal" involved some of the leading figures in American popular music. Rose, an inductee of the Songwriters Hall of Fame, was a Broadway producer and nightclub owner during the 1930s, as well as a lyricist with tunes such as "Me and My Shadow" and "It's Only a Paper Moon" to his credit. His prolific songwriting partner Mort Dixon, also an inductee of the Songwriters Hall of Fame, is perhaps best known for the lyrics to "Bye Bye Blackbird." Harry Warren wrote more than eight hundred songs in a long career that saw him nominated eleven times for an Academy Award for best song.

more liberally than anywhere else in North America." Even when other provinces began to legalize booze again during the 1920s and began opening government liquor stores, public drinking in bars and nightclubs remained illegal. In Ontario, for example, it was July 1934 before taverns or beverage rooms opened and in Nova Scotia and New Brunswick they did not arrive until 1948 and 1961 respectively. Not so in Montreal, where visitors looking for entertainment found dozens of nightspots – dance pavilions, clubs, theatres and ballrooms – catering to all tastes and every budget.

Montreal's reputation was enhanced by its location as a major railway hub with connections to large American cities like New York, Chicago and Boston. A small but significant black population consisting largely of train porters and their families lived close by the major rail stations around St. Antoine Street, a neighbourhood that would become known as Little Burgundy. By the 1920s the black population of Little Burgundy numbered as many as three thousand people and the community had gained a reputation for its raucous nightlife featuring black entertainers from the US

and Canada, leading jazz musicians among them. (It was in this atmosphere that Canada's finest jazz musician, Oscar Peterson, spent his boyhood, learning to play the piano from his father who was a railway porter and amateur player himself.) The centre of this district was known as the Corner, the intersection of St. Antoine and Mountain streets, where several of the so-called "black clubs" were situated, most notably Rockhead's Paradise Café and, a bit later, the Club St Michel. "You knew you were in show biz when you were working at Rockhead's Paradise or the Café [sic] St Michel," recalled one musician who arrived on the scene in the mid-1930s, just after prohibition ended. "It was like transporting yourself to Harlem."

Rockhead's Paradise was owned by Rufus Rockhead, a black railway porter originally from Jamaica. According to John Gilmore, Rockhead and other porters used to smuggle liquor on the trains between Montreal and Chicago during prohibition. Perhaps it was money he made from this illicit traffic that allowed Rockhead to leave his job and in 1928 set up his bar, the only Montreal club owned by a black person. Rockhead's was located in a nondescript three-storey building

A quintet of black musicians performs at the Club St Michel in Montreal. Like other clubs in Little Burgundy, it featured the latest jazz music for which the neighbourhood became well known.

■ The first recording studio in Canada opened in Montreal in 1909. It was owned by Emile Berliner – the German-born inventor of the gramophone who had moved to Canada in 1897 – and managed by his son Herbert. The Berliner Gramophone Company made recordings of local musicians and of touring acts that were visiting the city. The company trademark was illustrated by a picture of a small dog staring into the horn of a gramophone and the slogan "His Master's Voice." In 1918 Herbert Berliner established his own record company, Compo, in a Montreal suburb, and his brother Edgar took charge of the original operation. Initially Compo pressed recordings that originated in the US with American companies but eventually it had record labels of its own. The opportunity to record with the Compo and Berliner companies was another reason that Montreal was the entertainment capital of Canada during the 1920s. In 1924 the Berliner Gramophone Company was absorbed by the US-based Victor Talking Machine Company, which in turn was taken over by the Radio Corporation of America (RCA), creator of the RCA Victor record label. Compo survived as an independent Canadian company until it was bought by Decca Records in 1950.

that he had renovated to include a two-storey cabaret that attracted some of the biggest names in jazz and blues. Rockhead himself became a legend on the nightclub scene, known for his impeccable manners and the red flower he invariably wore in the lapel of his suit as he greeted each guest who entered his club. Another neighbourhood spot was the Terminal Club, across the street from the CPR's Windsor station. The Terminal was celebrated less for its music than as an after-hours joint where people came to party after the uptown clubs had closed. "The Terminal Club was the kind of place where anything could happen," recalled the musician Myron Sutton. "It was just a joint, but it was a well-known joint."

Sutton was a fixture on Montreal's frenetic nightclub scene. A reed player from Niagara Falls, Ontario, he had assembled a group called the Canadian Ambassadors, the first black jazz band in Canada, to play at the Gatineau Country Club near Ottawa in 1931. But Montreal was the place where jazz musicians wanted to be, not a sedate government town like Ottawa, and when the band moved there Sutton landed a gig opening a new club called Connie's Inn in

the city's east end. Boasting that it was "bringing Harlem to Montreal" (it borrowed its name from a club in Harlem), Connie's offered "the highest calibre of colored divertissement" according to one advertisement. The Ambassadors, billed as "the Colored Kings of Jazz," soon were acknowledged to be the pre-eminent black jazz ensemble in Montreal. "Uptown in the big hotels they had a different type of music than we had," Sutton later recalled. "They had ballroom music." By contrast, the Ambassadors played swing. "That's all we knew how to do. At that time, everybody liked swing, so they swung along with us!" Other east end clubs – centred around the corner of St. Catherine Street and the Main (Saint-Laurent Boulevard) – included Club Hollywood and the Chinese Paradise, mainly, but not exclusively, providing black entertainers for a white audience. Here the nightclubs coexisted with a flourishing red-light district where prostitution was, if not condoned by the authorities, at least overlooked. In 1925 Judge Louis Coderre, a former Conservative Member of Parliament, wrote a report bemoaning the widespread existence of prostitution and accusing the Montreal police of corruption.

BELOW Mynie Sutton and his Canadian Ambassadors were the first black jazz band in Canada when they formed in 1931. After the band broke up in 1939 Sutton, shown here third from the right, continued to play in smaller groups for a couple of years, then moved back to Niagara Falls where he worked as a welder until his retirement. He still played in area dance bands and was performing just two weeks before his death at the age of 78 in 1982.

RIGHT The Chinese Paradise was one of Montreal's east end cabarets where the atmosphere was a little less genteel than at the uptown supper clubs.

An array of decorative swizzle sticks that stirred the drinks at some of Montreal's prohibition-era nightspots.

"Vice stalks through our city with a hideous-ness and insolence that appear sure of impunity," he charged. "Prostitution itself ... operates and flourishes in Montreal like a commercial enterprise perfectly organized."

For visitors who were too timid or stuffy for the bohemian side of town there was always the safety and conventionality of the more staid uptown clubs on St. Catherine Street West. The most sophisticated of these was the Normandie Roof at the top of the Sheraton Mount Royal Hotel. The Normandie, an elegant supper club with dining and dancing to more mainstream music, also hosted live Saturday-night radio broadcasts from "America's Most Beautiful Room" (according to its publicity), featuring the Jack Denny Orchestra. Several of the clubs around the city – Connie's Inn, the Lido, the Roseland Ballroom, and others – took their names from famous New York and Parisian nightspots, signalling to visitors the class of entertainment that was on offer. This glamorous nightlife, called by one writer "the golden age of Montreal night clubs," fuelled by liquor and driven by the new music, continued into the 1950s. But it was kickstarted three decades earlier by prohibition and the opportunity that Quebec's relaxed liquor laws provided.

■ LIQUOR TOURISM WAS JUST ONE OF THE impacts that prohibition had on Canada, and by no means the most important one. Far more significant were the negative results, chiefly the level of corruption that prohibition introduced into Canadian public life. Probably no other government policy in the country's history did as much to debase the society it was intended to improve. Thousands of public officials – police officers, border guards, customs and temperance agents – took bribes to facilitate the illegal trade in booze. Others became traffickers themselves. Farmers built illegal stills in their barns; fishermen used their boats to smuggle liquor; unemployed young men found jobs doing the heavy lifting for the mob bosses who controlled the trade. Doctors and pharmacists became bootleggers. Criminals became folk heroes; ordinary people became criminals. Neighbours were encouraged to spy on one another and communities were honey-combed with informants. In 1921 the *Carleton Sentinel* newspaper of Woodstock, New Brunswick, editorialized that "the present effort of enforcement breeds a spy system that is repulsive; it creates an army of dishonest employees and a senseless bu-reaucracy. Say what you like about it the whole affair is a farce..." Legitimate manu-facturers of spirits and beer, some of them among the leading corporations in the country, provided product to vicious gang-sters who, as they knew, were distributing it illegally in the United States and also rerouting it back into Canada for domestic consumption, all in the name of inflating their profits. Politicians lined their own pockets and their parties received huge donations from the liquor interests to ignore the obvious flaws in the system of enforcement. Not to mention the tax rev-enues that flowed into government coffers. (The provinces profited as well; Nova Scotia, to take just one example, received more than one million dollars during a three-year period in the mid-1920s by taxing the sale of liquor for medical and other specialist purposes.) As an example of how little the law was observed, the *Regina Leader* newspaper estimated in 1923 that there were twenty thousand illicit stills operating in Saskatchewan

The front page of the *Toronto Globe and Mail*, January 7, 1920, announces the discovery by a revenue inspector of a "gigantic still" hidden in a haystack on a farm near Grimsby, Ontario. According to the reporter, it was the largest illicit still ever seized in the province, capable of producing 90 gallons (340 litres) of moonshine a day. It was the second still found in the neighbourhood in four months and one of tens of thousands of illegal stills on farms across the country. Widespread lawbreaking was one of the unfortunate legacies of prohibition.

Booze was not the only illicit substance being trafficked during the 1920s. Here a group of Vancouver law-enforcement officials pose with a shipment of opium seized during a raid in Chinatown.

Judging by the vests stuffed with drugs being modelled by two of the officers, drug smugglers shared some of their clandestine techniques with the liquor smugglers.

Members of the 29th (Vancouver) Battalion, part of the Canadian Expeditionary Force in France, vote in the 1916 BC provincial election. This election included a referendum on prohibition in which overseas soldiers were allowed to participate. It was suspected that former premier Richard McBride, then serving as BC's agent general in London, played a role in "fixing" the military vote against prohibition. Regardless, the measure passed. It was one of many instances when the political system was manipulated for or against prohibition.

alone, "or one for every fifteen farms." In Vancouver in 1929 a liquor control board official reported that there were seven thousand active bootleggers.

It is not just with the benefit of hindsight that all these unintended consequences of prohibition are seen. Many Canadians recognized at the time that the law was seriously flawed. In 1923 a pamphlet published by the Moderation League of Manitoba argued that prohibition "destroys respect for law. It increases crime. It degrades and corrupts those who attempt to enforce it and those who – though naturally law-abiding – cannot honestly sympathize with its extreme character." *Maclean's* magazine described the noxious odour of corruption emanating from the corridors of government: "Politicians and procurers, servants of the Government and prostitutes, graft in public places high and low, inefficiency almost unparalleled, are intermixed in a nauseous mess, comparable in gravity to nothing else previously been placed before a nose-holding and well-nigh despairing citizenry."

It is little wonder, therefore, that politicians began looking for alternatives to the policy that had turned out to be such a mistake. There was no going back to the free and easy days of open consumption; moderation was the new watchword. Some form of control was going to remain, but the question was how much. Saskatchewan had pioneered the idea of government-owned liquor dispensaries in 1915 and though it was a short-lived experiment the idea caught on in the 1920s as a middle ground between full-blown prohibition and the open bar. British Columbia was the first jurisdiction to opt for government control. In a plebiscite on October 20, 1920, voters overwhelmingly endorsed an end to prohibition and the introduction of government-controlled sales of alcohol. As a result, on June 15, 1921, the first public liquor stores opened. One by one the other provinces followed suit during the decade. Government control was not just a recognition that prohibition was failing. The new policy was expedient but it was also profitable for governments. Prohibition had turned out to be very expensive to enforce. With its repeal, taxes and profits from liquor sold at the public stores went directly into government treasuries instead of being lost to bootleggers. In BC, for example, profits from the new stores

■ During the 1920s, most provinces replaced prohibition with some form of government-controlled sale of alcoholic beverages. The outlier was Prince Edward Island, the first to introduce prohibition and the last to repeal it. These are the dates when prohibition ended in the provinces:

Quebec • 1919
British Columbia • 1921
Yukon • 1921
Manitoba • 1923
Alberta • 1924
Saskatchewan • 1925
New Brunswick • 1927
Ontario • 1927
Nova Scotia • 1930
Prince Edward Island • 1948

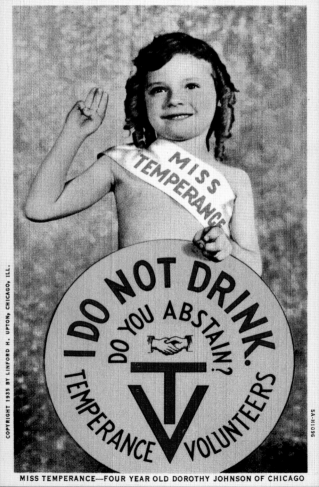

MISS TEMPERANCE

I DO NOT DRINK.
DO YOU ABSTAIN?
TEMPERANCE VOLUNTEERS

5A-H1096

MISS TEMPERANCE—FOUR YEAR OLD DOROTHY JOHNSON OF CHICAGO

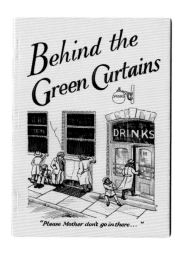

were running at about $2 million a year by the late 1920s. Within six months of Ontario introducing public liquor stores in 1927 the government was running a budgetary surplus.

In their operations, government stores reflected the lingering aftertaste of prohibition. Local liquor control boards went out of their way to discourage consumption. Retail outlets were few and far between and their hours of operation were restricted. They were badly lit inside and not well marked outside. In BC customers had to acquire a permit from the provincial police, then present it to a clerk who would fill the order. In at least two provinces a customer could not carry away his or her purchase; bottles had to be delivered to the home of the purchaser. The quantity of liquor that could be purchased was limited and advertising was banned in some provinces. Buying alcohol from a government store turned out to be almost as furtive as buying from a bootlegger.

Government control of retail sales was only the first step in the process of deregulating consumption. The second step – gradual reopening of public drinking spots – took longer. In BC, for instance, the government held yet another plebiscite in 1924 asking if the public approved the sale of beer by the glass in licensed premises; it was already available legally in private clubs. The answer by a narrow margin was No. However, a majority of electoral districts had voted Yes and later in the year the legislature, as much out of impatience with the issue as on principle, approved beer by the glass. The following March the province's first hotel beer parlours opened. Once again a temperance ethos persisted. Patrons were not allowed to stand at a bar, or drink standing up at all. No food, hard liquor, entertainment or games were available, nothing to suggest that drinking might be enjoyable. Out of concern for their virtue, women were not allowed to enter; eventually a separate room was added to accommodate females drinking alone or with escorts. These cheerless, dimly lit watering holes remained the main venue for public drinking in the province for decades, as they did across the country as in province by province the sale of beer by the glass was allowed in beverage rooms of one sort or another. Canada had entered a post-prohibition period where public drinking was permitted but was still considered to be mildly disreputable, if not immoral.

Consumers in Windsor celebrate the lifting of prohibition in Ontario on June 1, 1927. Alcohol was now available from government-operated liquor stores. No longer did people have to feign an illness to obtain a doctor's prescription, or risk imprisonment by buying from a bootlegger. Still, it was another seven years before licensed beverage rooms reopened in the province.

■ ADMITTING THE MANY WAYS THAT prohibition failed, there remains an argument to be made that it did succeed in its primary purpose: to reduce excessive drinking and the social dysfunction that often accompanies it. James H. Gray, in his classic study *Booze*, was adamant that prohibition was a success. Pooh-poohing "the legendary failure of Prohibition," Gray suggested instead that "it not only ushered in the most law-abiding era in prairie history, it marked the end of the maleficent impact of wide-open boozing on urban family life." In Gray's view, cowardly governments abandoned a progressive and effective social policy because they were seduced by the promise of ever-expanding tax revenues from controlled liquor sales; in other words, they became little better than bootleggers. But the evidence for Gray's claim that prohibition reduced consumption is hard to come by. Historian Craig Heron looks at the statistics on consumption and public drunkenness during the 1920s and concludes that alcoholic behaviour had more to do with economic circumstances than repressive laws. When times were good, people drank more; when they weren't, they didn't. Prohibition or not,

people would find a way to drink if they wanted to and if they could afford to. And even if it is admitted that prohibition may have resulted in a moderate decline in consumption, given the unfortunate side effects of the law it is arguable that the cure was much worse than the disease.

Aside from the romance and glamour attached to the prohibition era – gangsters, rum-runners, bootleg gin and dancing girls – it has also become in the popular mind a teachable moment from the past, a cautionary tale about the impossibility of imposing a public policy that is not broadly endorsed by the public. After the debacle of prohibition, who ever again would be foolish enough to try to use the law to change widely accepted personal habits? Yet in many people's minds we are living now through another prohibition era and it is having just as injurious an impact on public safety and personal mores. This time it is the sale and use of so-called recreational drugs, particularly marijuana, that is being prohibited by federal law. People are being sent to jail for using banned substances that a growing number of Canadians believe to be harmless, or no more harmful than other legal substances such as alcohol

and tobacco. Those in favour of "legalizing drugs" – polls suggest that number may now be the majority in at least parts of the country – point to the failure of liquor prohibition as an example of the futility, and injustice, of trying to ban an activity that has widespread support in the community. Once again, public opinion seems to be running ahead of government action. Just as prohibition of alcohol created the rum-runner and the gangster, so drug prohibition has created business opportunities for the drug cartels and biker gangs. Many of the arguments in favour of the liberalization of drug laws are the same arguments that led to the end of liquor prohibition: reduced enforcement costs, reduced violence among criminal gangs, increased tax revenues for government, fewer citizens branded as criminals for engaging in what is essentially a harmless personal habit. Treat drugs like alcohol, the argument goes: regulate and tax. As the debate enters mainstream political discourse, Canadians may be surprised to find that after all these years prohibition yet again becomes a ballot-box issue.

"The Café-Concert," an 1878 oil painting by the French Impressionist artist Edouard Manet, depicts a scene from the Cabaret de Reichshoffen on the Boulevard Rochechouart in Paris. The painting captures both the sophistication and the tawdriness of its setting, where well-to-do gentlemen rubbed shoulders with women from less polite backgrounds. This was the moral environment that prohibition activists and supporters of temperance in Canada were convinced existed in bars and beer parlours, which is why they worked so diligently to regulate drinking habits long after prohibition itself had failed.

SOURCES

GENERAL

The sources from which I drew inspiration and information are listed below, under the relevant chapters, but a number of more general sources were also useful. The best and most comprehensive history of alcohol consumption in Canada, including the prohibition period, is Craig Heron, *Booze: A Distilled History* (Toronto: Between the Lines, 2003). The similarly titled *Booze: The Impact of Whisky on the Prairie West* (Toronto: Macmillan of Canada, 1972), by James H. Gray, focuses on Western Canada; despite being more than forty years old, it is as entertaining and authoritative as the day it was written. The most recent account of the prohibition era in the United States is Daniel Okrent, *Last Call: The Rise and Fall of Prohibition* (New York: Scribner, 2010). Okrent's book formed the basis of Ken Burns's 2011 television documentary, *Prohibition*. Also useful were James H. Morrison and James Moreira, eds., *Tempered by Rum: Rum in the History of the Maritime Provinces* (Porters Lake, NS: Pottersfield Press, 1988) and Cheryl Krasnick Warsh, ed., *Drink in Canada: Historical Essays* (Montreal: McGill-Queen's University Press, 1993).

CHAPTER ONE

The description of the career of Roy Greenaway relies on his memoir, *The News Game* (Toronto: Clarke, Irwin & Co., 1966), and his essay collection, *Open House*, W.A. Deacon and Wilfred Reeves, eds. (Ottawa: Graphic Publishers, 1931), along with selected articles from the *Toronto Daily Star*. For the history of the *Star* I consulted Ross Harkness, *J.E. Atkinson of the Star* (Toronto: University of Toronto Press, 1963), supplemented by Douglas (George) Fetherling, *The Rise of the Canadian Newspaper* (Toronto: Oxford University Press, 1990) and Paul Rutherford, *The Making of the Canadian Media* (Toronto: McGraw-Hill Ryerson, 1978). The prohibition era in the Windsor, Ontario, area is brought vividly to life in the thirtieth anniversary edition of Marty Gervais, *The Rumrunners: A Prohibition Scrapbook* (Emeryville, ON: Biblioasis, 2009). Reverend Spracklin is the subject of Mark Bourrie, "Demon Rum," *Canada's History* (Aug.–Sept. 2011): pp. 18–25. Other useful sources for this episode include Gerald A. Hallowell, *Prohibition in Ontario, 1919–1923* (Ottawa: Ontario Historical Society, 1972); Philip P. Mason, *Rumrunning and the Roaring Twenties: Prohibition on the Michigan-Ontario Waterway* (Detroit: Wayne State University Press, 1995); and Peter Oliver, *Public & Private Persons: The Ontario Political Culture 1914–1934* (Toronto: Clarke, Irwin & Co., 1975).

CHAPTER TWO

Prohibition in Canada (Toronto: Ontario Branch of the Dominion Alliance, 1919) by Ruth Elizabeth Spence is a comprehensive account of the movement to ban alcohol up to the end of World War I, told from the point of a view of a zealous supporter. The role of the tavern in colonial life is described in Julia Roberts, *In Mixed Company: Taverns and Public Life in Upper Canada* (Vancouver: UBC Press, 2009). The discussion of Joe Beef relies on Peter DeLottinville, "Joe Beef of Montreal: Working-Class Culture and the Tavern, 1869–1889," *Labour/Le Travail* 8/9 (Autumn/Spring 1981–82): pp. 9-40. Before prohibition there was temperance, a subject well covered in Jan Noel, *Canada Dry: Temperance Crusades before Confederation* (Toronto: University of Toronto Press, 1995). For the history of the WCTU, see Sharon Anne Cook, *"Through Sunshine and Shadow": The Woman's Christian Temperance Union, Evangelicalism, and Reform in Ontario, 1874–1930* (Montreal: McGill-Queen's University Press, 1995). Pierre Berton wrote about Father Chiniquy in *My Country: The Remarkable Past* (Toronto: McClelland and Stewart, 1976). The rise of full-blown prohibitionism is discussed by Graeme Decarie, "Something Old, Something New: Aspects of Prohibitionism in Ontario in the 1890s" in Donald Swainson, ed., *Oliver Mowat's Ontario* (Toronto: Macmillan, 1972): pp. 154–71; Gerald A. Hallowell, *Prohibition in Ontario, 1919-1923* (Ottawa: Ontario Historical Society, 1972); and Douglas L. Hamilton, *Sobering Dilemma: A History of Prohibition in British Columbia* (Vancouver: Ronsdale Press, 2004). Goldwin Smith's views were published as *Temperance Versus Prohibition: An Address on the Scott Act* (Toronto: C.B. Robinson, 1885), while Stephen Leacock's most forceful attack on prohibition was "The Tyranny of Prohibition" in *Living Age* (August 2, 1919), reprinted in Alan Bowker, ed., *The Social Criticism of Stephen Leacock: The Unsolved Riddle of Social Justice and Other Essays* (Toronto: University of Toronto Press, 1973). A fine biography of Nellie McClung is Mary Hallett and Marilyn Davis, *Firing the Heather: The Life and Times of Nellie McClung* (Saskatoon: Fifth House Publishers, 1993). The reference to Matthew Begbie is from Renisa Mawani, *Colonial Proximities: Crossracial Encounters and Juridical Truths in British Columbia, 1871-1921* (Vancouver: UBC Press, 2009).

CHAPTER THREE

The story of the Picariello clan is told in Frank W. Anderson, *The Rumrunners* (Edmonton: Folklore Publishing, 1991); James H. Gray, *Talk to My Lawyer! Great Stories of Southern*

Alberta's Bar & Bench (Edmonton: Hurtig Publishers, 1987); and Howard Palmer, with Tamara Palmer, *Alberta: A New History* (Edmonton: Hurtig Publishers, 1990). For the Bronfmans I relied on Gray's *Booze*; Peter C. Newman, *Bronfman Dynasty: The Rothschilds of the New World* (Toronto: McClelland and Stewart, 1978) and the same author's *Mavericks: Canadian Rebels, Renegades and Anti-Heroes* (Toronto: Harper-Collins, 2010); and Michael R. Marrus, *Mr. Sam: The Life and Times of Samuel Bronfman* (Toronto: Viking Penguin, 1991). Rocco Perri's career is detailed in James Dubro and Robin F. Rowland, *King of the Mob: Rocco Perri and the Women Who Ran His Rackets* (Toronto: Penguin Books, 1987) and Antonio Nicaso, *Rocco Perri: The Story of Canada's Most Notorious Bootlegger* (Toronto: John Wiley & Sons, 2004), as well as in Stephen Schneider, *Iced: The Story of Organized Crime in Canada* (Toronto: John Wiley & Sons, 2009). A useful account of the scandal in the customs department may be found in Dave McIntosh, *The Collectors: A History of Canadian Customs and Excise* (Toronto: NC Press Ltd., 1984). For smuggling across the Great Lakes, see Edward Butts, *Outlaws of the Lakes: Bootlegging and Smuggling from Colonial Times to Prohibition* (Toronto: Lynx Images, 2004); C.W. Hunt, *Booze Boats and Billions: Smuggling Liquid Gold!*, 2nd ed. (Belleville, ON: Billa Flint Publications, 2000; originally published McClelland and Stewart, 1988) and the same author's *Whisky and Ice: The Saga of Ben Kerr, Canada's Most Daring Rumrunner* (Toronto: Dundurn Press, 1995); and William Siener, "'A Barricade of Ships, Guns, Airplanes and Men': Arming the Niagara Border, 1920–1930," *The American Review of Canadian Studies*, v. 38, no. 4 (Winter 2008): pp. 429–50. The best source for the New Brunswick experience is B.J. Grant, *When Rum Was King* (Fredericton, NB: Fiddlehead Books, 1984). For Nova Scotia, see E.R. Forbes, "Prohibition and the Social Gospel in Nova Scotia" in *Atlantic Canada After Confederation* (*The Acadiensis Reader*, vol. 2), edited by P.A. Buckner and David Frank (Fredericton: Acadiensis Press, 1985): pp. 260–85.

CHAPTER FOUR

The context for rum-running on the Pacific Coast is described in Robert A. Campbell, *Demon Rum or Easy Money: Government Control of Liquor in British Columbia from Prohibition to Privatization* (Ottawa: Carleton University Press, 1991); Douglas L. Hamilton, *Sobering Dilemma: A History of Prohibition in British Columbia* (Vancouver: Ronsdale Press, 2004); and Ruth Price, "The Politics of Liquor in British Columbia, 1920–1928," MA thesis, Simon Fraser University, 1991. Stories of the individual rum-runners and their vessels rely on Ruth Greene, *Personality Ships of British Columbia* (West Vancouver: Marine Tapestry Publications, 1969); Fraser Miles, *Slow Boat on Rum Row* (Madeira Park, BC: Harbour Publishing, 1992); Eric Newsome, *Pass the Bottle: Rum Tales of the West Coast* (Nanaimo: Orca Book Publishers, 1995) and *The Case of the Beryl G* (Orca Book Publishers, 1989); and Marion Parker and Robert Tyrrell, *Rumrunner: The Life and Times of Johnny Schnarr* (Victoria: Orca Book Publishers, 1988). For the Seattle bootlegger Roy Olmstead, I relied mainly on Philip Metcalfe, *Whispering Wires: The Tragic Tale of an American Bootlegger* (Portland: Inkwater Press, 2007). The activities of the US Coast Guard are detailed in Malcolm F. Willoughby, *Rum War at Sea* (Washington, DC: Government Printing Office, 1964). The exploits of the Atlantic Coast rum-runners are detailed in Hugh H. Corkum, *On Both Sides of the Law* (Hantsport, NS: Lancelot Press, 1989) and in Geoff and Dorothy Robinson, *It Came by the Boatload: Essays on Rum Running* (Summerside, PEI: The Authors, 1984) and *The Nellie J. Banks*, 4th ed. (Summerside, PEI: The Authors, 1993). For a review essay about Atlantic rum-running, see C. Mark Davis, "Atlantic Canada's Rum Running Tradition," *Acadiensis*, vol. 14, no. 2 (Spring 1985): 147–56. For Saint-Pierre and Miquelon specifically, two books by J.P. Andrieux were very useful: *Prohibition and St. Pierre* (Lincoln, ON: W.F. Rannie, 1983) and *Rumrunners: The Smugglers from St. Pierre and Miquelon and the Burin Peninsula from Prohibition to Present Day* (St. John's, NL: Flanker Press, 2009). Another useful article is David J. McDougall, "The Origins and Growth of the Canadian Customs Preventive Service Fleet in the Maritime Provinces and Eastern Quebec, 1892–1932" in *The Northern Mariner/Le marin du nord*, vol. 5, no. 4 (Oct. 1995): 37–57.

CHAPTER FIVE

The story of the Prince of Wales Hotel is told in Ray Djuff, *High on a Windy Hill: The Story of the Prince of Wales Hotel* (Calgary: Rocky Mountain Books, 1999), while the Huntingdon Chateau is described in Robert McGee, "The Founding of the Huntingdon Chateau" in the *Journal of the Chateauguay Valley Historical Society* (1994: 1–16). Also useful is Herbert D.A. Donovan, *Fort Covington and Her Neighbours: A History of Three Towns* (New York: O'Hare Books, 1963). For the history of jazz I relied on John Gilmore, *Swinging in Paradise: The Story of Jazz in Montreal* (Montreal: Véhicule Press, 1988); Nancy Marrelli, *Stepping Out: The Golden Age of Montreal Night Clubs, 1925–1955* (Montreal: Véhicule Press, 2004); Mark Miller, *Such Melodious Racket: The Lost History of Jazz in Canada, 1914–1949* (Toronto: Mercury Press, 1997) and William Weintraub, *City Unique: Montreal Days and Nights in the 1940s and '50s* (Toronto: McClelland and Stewart, 1996). Robert Campbell, *Sit Down and Drink Your Beer: Regulating Vancouver's Beer Parlours 1925–1954* (Toronto: University of Toronto Press, 2001) describes the new regime of liquor control that succeeded prohibition.

CREDITS & PERMISSIONS

EVERY REASONABLE EFFORT HAS BEEN MADE to trace and contact all holders of copyright and to credit sources correctly. In the event of omission or error Douglas & McIntyre should be notified so that a full acknowledgment may be made in future editions.

AO	Archives of Ontario
ARHSJ	Archives of the Religious Hospitallers of Saint Joseph, Saint-Basile, NB
BCA	British Columbia Archives
CI	Corbis Images
CMC	Canadian Museum of Civilization
CU	Concordia University
CVA	City of Vancouver Archives
CW	City of Waterloo
CWM	Canadian War Museum
DHS	Detroit Historical Society
DN	Detroit News
GA	Glenbow Archives
GI	Getty Images
GS	GetStock
HMA	Hagley Museum and Archives
IM	International Metropolis
LAC	Library and Archives Canada
LOC	Library of Congress
MACM	My Al Capone Museum
MAUM	Musée acadien de l'Université de Moncton
MCM	McCord Museum
MOHAI	Museum of History & Industry
MUL	McGill University Library, Rare Books and Special Collections
MUN	Memorial University of Newfoundland, Maritime History Archive
NBM	New Brunswick Museum
NVMA	North Vancouver Museum & Archives
NYPL	New York Public Library
PANB	Provincial Archives of New Brunswick
PB	PBase

POC	Post-Intelligencer Collection, MOHAI
PSRA	Puget Sound Regional Archives
SAB	Saskatchewan Archives Board
SAVM	Service d'Archive de la Ville de Montréal
SMPM	Seattle Metropolitan Police Museum
TDHS	Tavistock and District Historical Society
TFRBL	Thomas Fisher Rare Book Library, University of Toronto
TGM	*The Globe and Mail* online collection
TLL	Toledo-Lucas Library
TMM	The Mariner's Museum
TPL	Toronto Public Library
TS	*Toronto Star*
USC	Univeristy of South Carolina
USCG	US Coast Guard
UW	University of Washington
UWL	University of Waterloo Library Archives and Rare Books
VM	VirtualMuseum.ca
VPM	Vancouver Police Museum
WSU	Wayne State University Walter P. Reuther Library
YCM	Yarmouth County Museum

COVER
CI BE047630

HALF-TITLE PAGE
GS 2223400023

TITLE PAGE
DN 39103475e

CONTENT PAGE
GI 123410470-10

CHAPTER ONE
p.6: AO 10015265; p.8: Courtesy of MACM; p.9: DN 39103451; p.11: DN 39103502e; p.12: TFRBL 6442207249 and 6442207197; p.13: GS 2083218365; p.14: GS *Toronto Star* Collection; p.15: GS 2079400487; p.16: DHS 2012044702 and 2012044700; p.17: DHS 2012044705, 2012044704, 2012044701, and 2012044703; p.18: IM 530op09; p.19: TS *Toronto Star* Front

Page Collection; p.20: LAC PA-069901; p.21: TFRBL 0001-4-0; p.22: TFRBL 6419929867, 6442210767, and 6419928463; p.23: TFRBL 6419929217, 6419928915, 6442200921, 6442211783, 6419930031, and 6887159341; p.24: MAUM 1995.399.A.B; p.25: DN 39103464E; p.26: DN 39103463E; p.27: top DN 39103467E; bottom DN 39103450E; p.28: TFRBL 6442214031, 6419924055, and 6419927053; p.28/29: TDHS 282; p.30: TLL 15026; p.31: DN 39103495E; p.33 DHS 2013085013; p.34: TPL PC-ON2075; p.35: LAC C-151590; p.36: GS 2081502729; p.37: DHS 2012046780; p.38: left GS 2218400384; centre left LOC LC-USZ62-97941; centre right DN 39103497E; right DN 39103441E.

CHAPTER TWO

p.40: GA NA-1751-5; p.42: LAC C-123164; p.43 top TFRBL 6419928651, bottom MCM V8752; p.44: LAC E008128929; p.45: BCA C-06025; p.46: BCA F-02562; p.47: MCM M995X.5.35.2; p.48: LAC C-089660; p.49: LAC E008300587; p.50: left LAC E010865573, right LAC E010865573-S1; p.51: MCM M930.51.1.87; p.52: MCM M930.50.6.5; p.53: left TFRBL 6442202955, top right TFRBL 6442206263, bottom right TFRBL 6442205065; p.54: MCM M930.50.8.123; p.55: TFRBL CAP00825; p.56: BCA D-07520; p.57: left TFRBL CAP02712, right NBM X12455; p.58: top TFRBL 6419924641, bottom TFRBL 6419930223; p.59: top left TFRBL 6500488859, top right TFRBL 6419926759, bottom TFRBL 6419927533; p.60: left LAC C-000066, right TFRBL CAP02685; p.61: MCM M988.182.152; p.62: LAC E008300582; p.63: BCA D-07410; p.64: left MCM M930.50.1.691, centre left MCM M930.51.1.365, centre right MCM M930.51.1.373, right MCM M930.51.1.375; p.65: LOC G99301908.B8; p.67: left LAC E010865575; p.68: NVMA 978.78.3; p.69 TFRBL RBD00427; p.70 TFRBL CAP00338; p.71: left

LAC E002505637-V6, right LAC E003641663-V8; p.72: left LAC PA-030212, right TFRBL CAP01390; p.74 left MCM M992.6.265.1-2, right GA NC-29-47; p.76: GA PA-3803-2; p.77: left LAC E008300581, right GA NA-450-1; p.78: GI 3097039, p.79: GA NA-1639-1; p.80: left CWM 19900076-819, right MUL WP1.F10.F2; p.81: MUL WP1.F11.F2; p.82: TFRBL 6442210047; p.83: top LAC PA-072527, bottom PA-072525; p.84: LAC E008748929-V8.

CHAPTER THREE

p.86: USCG Courtesy of the US Coast Guard; p.88: top BCA A-04474, bottom BCA D-09644; p.89: GA NA-1136-1; p.90: GA NA-3282-2; p.91: top GA NA-2899-10, bottom GA NA-2899-11; p.92: top TFRBL 6419925807, bottom TFRBL 6419927981; p.93: top left TFRBL 6419925857, middle left TFRBL 6887144497, bottom left TFRBL 6887139287, top right TFRBL 6887139919, middle right TFRBL 6419927679, bottom right TFRBL 6887157323; p.94: left TFRBL 6419926251, right TFRBL 6419926145; p.95: GA NA-1352-1; p.96: top GA NA-2180-6, bottom GS C2JEO7; p.97: CVA 480-215; p.98: HMA P20091015-002; p.99: top GA PA-3481-16, bottom GI 103000510; p.100: CI BE044586; p.101: WSU 75490-1; p.102: left TFRBL 6419927237, right TFRBL 6442208709; p.103: TGM; p.104: left GI 97939748; p.104/105: GI 97305282; p.106: GS 2081500479; p.108: WSU 74113-2-VMC; p.109: TGM; p.110: top CMC S2002-2953, bottom LAC PA-138867; p.111: LAC C-033995; p.112: WSU 63890-1-VMC; p.113: Courtesy Brian Osborne; p.114: top WSU 63903-1-VMC, bottom WSU 63902-1-VMC; p.115: GI 2669499; p.116: WSU 73811-1-VMC; p.118: top USCG Courtesy of the US Coast Guard, bottom DHS 2012044658; p.119: USCG Courtesy of the US Coast Guard; p.120: left LAC PA-125133, right top TFRBL 6442208241, right bottom TFRBL 6442208417; p.121: TFRBL 6442202449; p.122: Courtesy of ARHSJ AM559B; p.123: PANB MC215-MS3A12; p.124: SAB R-A7536; p.125: LAC C-005994.

CHAPTER FOUR

p.126: TMM apk22v15; p.128: PSRA 344800-1435; p.129: DHS 1964204002; p.131: SMPM Courtesy of the Seattle Metropolitan Police Museum; p.132: MOHI 1983.10.2020; p.133: top MOHI 1987.30.2, bottom POC 1986.5G.2269; p.134: TFRBL top 8654958887, bottom TFRBL 8654958939; p.135: CVA 99-3487; p.136: BCA F-02227; p.137: USCG 5-4-23N; p.138/139: LOC LC-USZ62-50082; p.139: LOC LC-USZ62-50081; p.140: CVA 99-3071; p.141: PB top left 116509887, top middle PB 116509895, top right PB 116509892, bottom PB 116509889; p.142: top TMM APK18v15, bottom TMM APK65v15; p.143: TMM APK77v15; p.144: TMM APK31v15; p.145: left, UWL seaar14s, right CW 84-2-24; p.146: top MUN PF001-H005B, bottom MUN PF001-H006A; p.147: TMM APK05v15; p.148: DHS 2012022508; p.149: top WSU 9732-1-VMC, bottom WSU 9731-VMC; p.150: USCG CG-8031; p. 151 CI U104925ACME; p.153: USCG G-APA-04-19-23; p.154: WSU 23976-VMC.

CHAPTER FIVE

p.156: GI 123410470; p.158: CVA 99-355; p.159: X.2810; p.160: top GA M-1448-1; p.161: GA NA-4030-12; p.163: top left CU P019Sutton14, bottom left CU P019Sutton14A, right CU P019Sutton27; p.164: NYPL 169937; p.165: USC Courtesy of the University of South Carolina, Irvin Department of Rare Books & Special Collections; p.167: CU P004Gilmore-8; p.169: CU bottom P004-02-73; p.169: top SAVM Z-42. VM94, bottom CU P019Sutton-3; p.170: CU P078Jazz-2-0; p.172: CU P078Jazz-2-0; p.173: TGM; p.174: VPM P03717; p.175: CVA LP202; p.176: CI LW002406; p.177: GA NA-2629-13; p.178: WSU 9734-VMC.

1 2 3 4 5 — 18 17 16 15 14

Cataloguing data available from Library
and Archives Canada
ISBN 978-1-77162-037-6 (paper)
ISBN 978-1-77162-038-3 (ebook)

DOUGLAS & McINTYRE (2013) LTD.
P.O. Box 219, Madeira Park, BC, V0N 2H0
www.douglas-mcintyre.com

Edited by Helen Godolphin and Mark Stanton
Image research and selection by Roberto Dosil
Cover and text design by Roberto Dosil
Printed in China

We gratefully acknowledge the financial
support of the Government of Canada through
the Canada Book Fund and the Canada
Council for the Arts, and from the Province of
British Columbia through the BC Arts Council
and the Book Publishing Tax Credit.